INDIVIDUAL
POWER

INDIVIDUAL POWER

RECLAIMING YOUR CORE, YOUR TRUTH, AND YOUR LIFE

BARBARA ROSE

The Rose Group
(in association with Trafford Publishing)
Coral Springs, Florida

Individual Power:
Reclaiming Your Core, Your Truth, and Your Life

The Rose Group
Publishing Division
7667 W. Sample Road, #207
Coral Springs, Florida 33065
www.borntoinspire.com

Trafford Publishing Service
Suite 6E, 2333 Government St.
Victoria, BC, Canada V8T 4P4
www.trafford.com

Contact the author through her Web site:
www.borntoinspire.com

Text editing by Lisa A. Smith <www.writingatwork.com>

Text and cover design and layout by Robert Goodman, Silvercat®,
San Diego, California <info@silvercat.com>

ISBN 0-97414-570-X

In memory of my dearest Grandma Rose

Thank you for giving me roots and wings, for believing in me when the rest of the world turned away, and for loving me unconditionally. Thank you for making so many of my dreams come true. Your love still sustains me. I will love you and keep your memory alive each day for the rest of my life.

To my parents

Thank you for believing in me, for healing the past, for loving me unconditionally, and for cheering me while others laugh. I love you, and I am proud to be your daughter.

To my children, Kelly and Michael

You are the gifts of my life. Thank you for your patience and understanding every time I had to work; for your comforting hugs every time I cried, and for teaching me how to be a kid again. Thank you for being the beautiful children that you are. I love you with all my heart. I am the luckiest mom on Earth to have you for my children. Always follow your heart. I am behind you all the way!

To Alan

I found the truth in my writings because of you.
This book would never have been possible without you.
Thank you, soul mate, for the healing and the growth.

To my editor, Lisa A. Smith

I know God sent you to me.
Thank you for your profound work.

To you, my new friend
You have only just begun!

CONTENTS

FOREWORD

I've just returned from a great lunch with an old friend. What made it so great? We could let our guard down to explore our deepest personal issues and try to figure out how emotional issues can play out for the best. What a wonderful feeling I was left with!

That same feeling comes to me as I read Barbara Rose's superb book, *Individual Power*. When a spirit sings clearly and beautifully of life's inner struggles with truth and love, a tone too exquisite for words can be heard. This is the sound of Ms. Rose's book. *Individual Power* is like no other book ever written: on the one hand it is so personally revealing, yet on the other hand it is selfless and universal in its perspective. Each section rings true to those who have succeeded inwardly with an open heart.

At this time of rapid technological advances, we often lose sight of the value of inner soul development. We may feel a distaste for the humdrum of daily obligations and pressing routines. Yet we jump through the hoops without too much protest. Meanwhile, the inner spirit may languish for lack of caring. Ms. Rose's book is the balm that waters the thirsty soul with so much nurturing energy.

As the author of four books and more than sixty articles, I've certainly done my share of pondering the true nature of human growth. But I stand aside and salute Ms. Rose's talents with words and ideas, not to mention her facility with spiritual dimensions. "For a relationship to last," she writes, "it must be built on truth." How fundamentally simple yet powerful in its proclamation! We know this to be self-evident when we see the words, yet how many lies may have crept into our most significant relationship under the seductive guise of avoiding unnecessary conflict!

This book is not to be read. It is to be gently inhaled into your deepest soul. It changed my perspective on human relationships. It graced me with more confidence to make things work out even when they seemed beyond my control. I'm usually skeptical about advice on human relations. But Ms. Rose comes from such an authentic, sincere, and humble-yet-powerful position that her words broke through my guard like air flowing through an open window. You're blessed to have this book in your hands. I hope you'll share it with your dear ones.

David Ryback, Ph.D.
Author of *Love, Sex, and Passion for the Rest of Your Life*

PREFACE

$\mathcal{F}$or many people there comes a certain moment in the deepest chapter of their life when all they have ever known, valued, understood, and strived for vanishes. This is usually known as the darkest hour or the darkness before the dawn.

Such has been the case in my life and in the lives of many whose paths have crossed mine. Through this book, your path and mine will come together; soon, you will understand why.

Why is it that the fabric of our reality, of our very existence, seems to hinge on people or situations that, in the end, truly have no power to create our lives for us? Why does life often seem so meaningless? Have you ever felt that you've lost the true core of your individual power?

What, exactly, is this thing I call individual power?

Is it money, a relationship, a career? The latest car, biggest home, or newest diamond watch? A corporate takeover or political move? No. Yet in our twenty-first-century society, many – perhaps most – would have you believe that your very life, livelihood, happiness, well-being, and future security hinge on any one or a number of those things.

Perhaps someone – your spouse, your employer – has led you to buy into the false view that your happiness or security lies in his hands.

Well, as a woman who was born into wealth, traveled the world, experienced the finest of life on planet Earth only to have it all stripped away, I learned. I learned there are masses of people who do not have a voice, who cannot speak out for themselves, largely due to lack of money and, thus, lack of perceived power.

I learned, in an unjust legal custody battle, how money buys justice while it shields the truth. My eyes opened during my darkest hour. They opened to the oppressed, the grief stricken, the homeless, and the hungry. No longer was I among the elite, the in crowd. Now I was among the masses, and it was simultaneously an empowering and a tragic position to find myself in. So I realized people, you, need a voice. Not an advocate, not another political representative who will strip you of even more of your individual power. No. People, you, need your own voice. With that voice you can reclaim your power and create the life of your own choosing, independent of the belief system you have bought into and, in most cases, in spite of it.

My purpose in this book is to hit home with you, my new friend, my reader. To hit home with truth that will engage your mind, challenge your perceptions, and stir your soul into uncharted territory. Then you, too, can awaken and reclaim your very own self.

As a result, the consciousness of humanity shall be raised: your consciousness, your light, your purpose, and your responsibility to yourself and to all others.

So in this journey, let the truth sink in, and fear not a change in your paradigm, for it has been your paradigm that has swallowed up the courage to uplift yourself far beyond where even you have told yourself you can go.

No, this book will not soothe you. It will challenge and inspire you to blaze your own trail. As a result, your light shall be a beacon for those whose lives you touch. And what a profound concept that is: to touch the lives of those dearest to you not by doing more but by being more!

So come. Let us go to a place we have rarely visited, that place of true individual power.

PART I

PERSONAL EMPOWERMENT

1

INDIVIDUAL GROWTH
AND RESPONSIBILITY

*Taking Your Life
Into Your Own Hands*

Surely there must be a way for you to have all you desire, to be all you can imagine, without having to undergo untold emotional misery. Why should people have to suffer in order to earn their joy? Why must people think that to achieve success they have to struggle? Whoever told you that life is hard, difficult, a daily grind? Whose idea did you buy into when you learned "this is the hand you've been dealt," and this is all there is?

Is that what you believe? Do you truly think your life was meant to be one heartache after another? One loss after another? Illness? Disaster? Chaos? Catastrophe? What about "paying your dues"? Suffering at the bottom for untold years, just to be able to buy food for yourself and your family? Who exactly has lied to you this way?

Well, if you want to know, if you truly want an edge up on the competition, then I have a bit of news for you: Life is meant to be filled with absolute joy. It is meant to be a pleasure.

Work, I have learned, is an exciting, exhilarating adventure, a passionate process in which people do their very best

*because they truly love every moment of what they are
doing!*

HOW TO TURN THE FALSE VIEWS AROUND

Individual growth, on the other hand, is a struggle. It is not easy
to replace old, ingrained, negative patterns with new views, beliefs, habits, and courses of action. Yet, individual growth can be
one of the brightest adventures in your life. For you do get to look
back and see just how far you have come. And this is what I have
found to be so exciting.

But how do you start? Well, with an idea. A simple idea of exactly how you want to be. How you want to live. What kind of
person you wish to become. Which traits you want to change.
And which traits you wish to substitute for the old ones.

If I told you that you, yes, *you*, can be *anything* you desire, have
any kind of life, the life *you* choose, would you believe me? This is
the truth.

I cannot tell you how exhilarating it feels for me to be at the
absolute bottom of life in American society and watch myself create my way up to the top out of sheer will, vision, and determination. Of course, pure passion backs my climb as I undertake to
reach every one of my goals.

*The beginning of personal growth is the idea of who, exactly,
in fine detail, you wish to become.*

Visualize your ideal you, and mentally create a picture of your
dream life.

Once you have envisioned this in your mind, keep it there.
And know – believe – that if your motives are pure, if your desire
is to grow and to better yourself, then nothing in this universe can
hold you back.

Oh, your husband? You would never stay with someone who
cuts you down, who hinders your individual growth and undermines your progress.

Your wife? Perhaps she must stop depending on you, so she can start to see the value of independence.

Your employer? Sorry. You'll just have to find another one or start your own business. It doesn't matter if your business is babysitting or selling fruit. When you're your own boss, no other person can dictate to you.

Now, the key to picturing your ideal self is to get so excited about creating your highest vision of self that you will be able to create it without the permission, approval, or validation of others. If there are people in your life who make fun of you or put you down or laugh at you, then simply tell them nothing. You do not *owe* your neighbors, friends, or family members any explanation regarding your individual growth. Your personal goals and dreams, your efforts to create the highest vision of yourself are none of their business. I learned something a long time ago: never take advice from people whose shoes you would never want to be in. It is precisely those people who are miserable with their own lives and with themselves, those people who never fulfilled their own highest potential, who will mock and make fun of others who are about to embark on turning their own dream into reality. You are here in this life to be and to bring out from within yourself, in every area of personal expression, all you truly are. You are able to picture your ideal self because every single attribute you wish to have already exists within you and awaits its full expression in your life.

CREATING A FANTASY OR A NEW REALITY?

Once you have envisioned all you wish to become, you just might think that it is such a fantasy, so out of the realm of logical possibility, that discouragement may soon replace passion and excitement.

Your highest and most exciting vision of self is paramount to your success, to finding the joy completely from within and not from any other person, place, or thing.

In the beginning, you will feel, just as I once did, as if you are standing at the bottom of Mt. Everest looking up and thinking, "No way!" But you know that saying: "The journey of a thousand miles begins with a single step." And you know that the days, weeks, and months are going to go by anyway. So why not use that time productively to get where you want to go and become who you really want to be rather than settling for any aspect of your life that causes you misery in your daily existence.

That misery may permeate your entire life or just one part of it. You could love your spouse but hate your work, or vice versa. No matter what part of yourself you wish to change, no matter how big or small a job it is, the only thing that matters is that you begin a brand-new day with the idea of a brand-new you. The *you* you would love to see yourself become.

Now, did you ever notice that if there is something in your life you need to take care of, you are usually given enough time to take care of it? And did you ever notice that when you procrastinate, when you put off doing what you need to do, you wind up having to do it anyway, only it becomes a more urgent task?

When I did not take the initiative to make the changes I needed to make for me, somehow, somewhere along the line, something would happen, leaving me with absolutely no choice. Like getting a parking ticket and putting off paying the fine. Then procrastinating on renewing my car registration. Then forgetting to buy stamps to mail off my car insurance. I had the time; I just put it off. Then, those red and blue lights chased my car when I was driving to work in a hurry. I found myself getting four tickets: for a suspended license, failure to pay a traffic ticket, an expired car registration, and cancelled auto insurance. The officer was kind enough not to take me to jail. Instead, she took away my license and told me that if I got caught driving, I would certainly go to jail. She said my license could be reinstated if I just took care of the tickets. Well, within two hours, I cleared up the whole mess: Car insurance intact. Tickets paid. Registration renewed. License reinstated. And this is a *minor* example.

My point is that we *do* have ample opportunity to take care of ourselves, our lives, and our responsibilities on our *own initiative*, before the consequences of procrastination create conditions that leave us no choice at all.

It took me a few decades, but I finally realized that I could have achieved personal responsibility for my life, happiness, and existence a lot sooner if I hadn't been so lazy or dependent on others: dependent on their financial help, opinions, encouragement, permission, and validation.

WHEN YOU LOSE IT ALL

I am the mother of two special children. My son and my daughter bring me far more joy than I gave my mother when I was a teenager. When my children were babies in diapers, I was financially dependent on my husband. He earned and controlled the money. I was a stay-at-home mom.

So when I got divorced, he was supposed to pay child support. I'm sure he was not the first man who went to jail for failure to pay, nor will he be the last. He refused to take care of his responsibility; but so did I.

I did not seek to become financially independent. It was far too easy to depend on his money to raise my children. I also depended on my grandmother, who was supportive. As I watched myself depending on others for my financial survival, I saw that my self-esteem was pretty low. It's hard to feel empowered when you need the help of others to buy food and pay the rent.

But as the years passed – six of them – I continued to depend completely on Grandma and my ex-husband for money. I did get ill; I believe it was due to severe stress. In retrospect, how could I not feel stress when I was so dependent on others?

Then my grandmother became ill and needed all her money for her own health care; she could no longer help me financially. When I phoned to ask my ex-husband to please pay his child support in the amount stipulated in our divorce papers, he hung up on me.

So there I was, in 1996, with two small children to feed and a turn-off notice for every utility. I was a sitting duck.

I was a good mother. I still am. I never once hit or abused my children in any way. I believe in positive reinforcement, not negative punishment.

But I was also still needy and dependent. So I filed an emergency motion, pro se, to the court for the original amount of child support. I filed on my own because I did not have the money to hire an attorney.

When my ex-husband received his copy of the papers, he did have money for an attorney, and he promptly filed a custody suit, to take the children away from me. He simply did not want to give me money.

I was in a complete state of shock when I was served with the papers. I truly believed he did not have a case; no chance in this world of winning. I had done nothing wrong: no drugs, no alcohol, no crime, no abuse, no neglect. I was just financially strapped. So I truly believed a judge would not, or could not, take my children away from me.

I had yet to learn about the American justice system, where money wins and poor innocence loses. It was a brutal lesson. I saw the games that go on behind the scenes in some of our courtrooms. Judges, who once practiced law, may have friendships with certain attorneys with whom they have longtime professional associations, not to mention memberships in the same golf and country clubs. And judges may not look favorably on people who represent themselves.

I felt as if I was reduced to pond scum instead of receiving respect for being a good mother. No, the ex-husband, who had gone to jail for failure to pay child support, was the one who garnered all the respect. He had a top attorney; he could afford to take the children to Disney World; and he could buy them computers, nice clothes, and new bedroom sets. In other words, he could put on a great show for the court because he had money.

The money game was being played, and I was marked as the loser before I could even get started. My innocence was treated like guilt: with disdain. Money was treated like royalty: with respect. Bottom line, I lost primary custody of my two children.

Shortly thereafter, I lost my soul. My daily existence was reduced to self-loathing. I remained feeling victimized for about two years.

What triggered this misery? How did I rise above it? What can you learn from my mistakes? Read on.

THE CORE LESSONS OF LOSS

My dependency, my lack of financial responsibility cost me my children, and I hated myself to the core for this. For if I had pushed myself to be financially self-sufficient, I would have had the joy of raising my children through the years.

Of course, the choice was mine. I did have the opportunity to learn how to support myself, yet it was much easier (I thought then) to have Grandma's help. Yes, the judicial system lacks justice, but the blame must ultimately fall on me.

In what way can I grow? For once I grow, then I can take the seeds of my greatest tragedy and turn them into good for our society.

It all starts with me. Surely it would be easy to remain a poor, railroaded victim of American injustice, forever blaming a corrupt legal system for my woes and heartache. It would be much harder to make a fresh start and actually do something to change my situation.

During the two years I remained a victim, emotionally brutalized by the pain of injustice and loss, I began to see others who were also lost. Lost in a sea of the masses in our society. Lost in perceived lack of power. Lost in their false views of who they were. What most people, including myself back then, and perhaps even you today, never realize is that

The moment you decide exactly where you are going, that is the precise moment your entire life changes course.

Understandably, despair overcame me. But we all have despair. Every one of us has a story. We each have heartache. And, as I said in the preface of this book, it is simultaneously the most tragic and the most empowering place to be.

TURNING TRAGEDY INTO SELF-EMPOWERMENT

How can tragedy be empowering? Because it brings you to the moment of truth, the real truth, the truth that ultimately sets you free. Through the darkness of tragedy, you reach the dawn, which is the moment you decide it will never be this way again.

This is the moment when you change the entire direction of the rest of your life because you refuse to go back to where you have just been.

The fact is that many people, most people, have to endure untold heartache and tragedy before they wake up, before they realize they have a choice. The direction of your life is in your hands alone. Blame for where you are in this life cannot be placed on any other. When we stop blaming and start creating the vision we want to see fulfilled, we then feel authentically empowered from within.

As I said earlier, I did have ample opportunity to take care of what I needed to, but I thought laziness and stagnation was so much easier. Obviously I thought wrong. Personal stagnation breeds self-hate. It feeds on negativity. It seeks injustice. It does not carry the exuberance, passion, and joy that accompany the search for new, better, and brighter paths and the striving toward fulfillment of your deepest dreams. Taking your life into your own hands and turning it around entirely, all of your own choosing, is an extraordinary adventure. Yes, it is scary. Change is always scary. But it is also thrilling. And after a while, you get used to the new, better way. And the old ways become as uncomfortable as shoes that are three sizes too small.

So why do millions and millions of people suffer beneath the dictates of their own false views or the dictates of others who they wrongly perceive as holding their happiness or even their very survival in their hands?

Why must you undergo any unpleasant circumstance that is not of your own choosing?

Why, I ask you, are you holding on to something or someone, or some position in your career or in society that is not bringing you absolute joy? Who, besides your very own self, tells you that you don't have a choice?

This is your biggest lie to yourself.
You do have a choice.

I tell you this boldly, straight to your face: Each day that you hold on to this person or situation that does not bring you joy, you choose it as your reality.

If you let go, if you walk away, if you no longer allow that person or situation into your life – then you are free!

And you know what part of *your* life this pertains to.

Did you ever have a job you hated? Did you ever just hang in there because you needed the money to pay the bills? Did anyone ever suggest that you simply get another job? Were you afraid to let go, in spite of your misery? You held on to your unhappiness because you bought into the belief that you had to. You believed you didn't have a choice, right? Well, suppose you got fired from that job. What then? Would you die? No, you'd get another job. Perhaps a better one! Perhaps one in which you made enough to buy a new pair of shoes after you paid your bills.

Here's the point:

If you are not happy,
then your situation is not in your best interest.

You can come up with every rationalization known to human-kind, but the bottom line is that it starts with you.

Change can begin only when you decide it can.

HOW TO DISCOVER YOUR LIFE PURPOSE

You have a responsibility to yourself. There is a job you're here on Earth to do. Do you even know what it is?

Do you have any clue
about what your purpose in this life is?

That is your responsibility as an individual. Your first responsibility to yourself, to your family, and to your society is to find out what you are on this Earth to do. Until you figure this out, you will continue to be unhappy.

I can't tell you why you are here, but I will tell you why you are not.

You are not here to placate others.
You are not here to work for meager wages while you make
the elite few richer and richer.
You are not here to degrade yourself, or to take abuse, or to
destroy your last shred of self-esteem.
You are not here to suffer, and you are not a sinner no mat-
ter how many mistakes you have made in your life.

If you really want to make a difference in this world, for yourself or for others, you must begin with the understanding and realization of what it is you are here to do. And to find that realization, you must look first in your heart.

What brings you complete, passionate joy?

I'll share a secret with you that is not so secret. One of my favorite role models is Oprah Winfrey. I once heard her say on television that what she does comes as naturally to her "as breathing." In other words, her work *is* her joy. That explains why she is so great at it; that explains her success and her ability to reach out and *truly* touch the lives of others in such positive ways. So take a tip from Oprah.

Whatever you love to do
will be as natural to you as breathing.

It can be baking, banking, or sewing. Driving, flying, or boating. It does not matter what it is; the only thing that matters is that you absolutely love doing it. You should be so passionate about your work that you can't believe you will actually earn money doing it.

That is your life purpose.

One of the ironies of life is that so many people search outside themselves to find their life purpose rather than seeking the joy within.

When you are passionate about your work, you may earn great sums of money. But your life purpose is not to accumulate massive wealth and possessions. Suppose you had every material thing you desired. *Then* what would you want to do? Travel? Perhaps you can, as a career! Shop? Do you really want to shop? OK, you can *own* the stores. Then what?

When you search outside yourself for your joy, you become a victim. You get caught in a trap: to validate your very being you have to keep those "things" in your life.

That is not joy. That is hoarding.

Hoarding breeds negativity and low self-worth.

When you derive your inner happiness from any outside thing or from status, your joy is no longer your own. It belongs to that which is outside of you.

Many people have acquired vast fortunes of material wealth only to lose it all. Some commit suicide. Others simply start the process of finding their joy all over again. The reason people lose their fortunes is so they can learn that their outer, material success is not the basis on which to validate themselves or their self-worth.

When people who are stripped of all their material wealth can still say they love themselves, love their lives, love those who are dearest to them, and love the process of life – those are the people who are truly doing what they came into this life to do. They are *being* rather than having.

If you believe that your life, your value as a human being is sustained or depleted by what you own, what you drive, who you travel with, the title on your business card, or any other sign of status, then you are living a fallacy. You are blind to your own essence and thus to your important purpose on this planet.

HOW TO TURN TRAGEDY INTO TRIUMPH

We have all undergone tragedy. Perhaps there is a reason why you chose a particular life lesson – a particular tragedy – to help yourself grow and become who you were meant to be. Perhaps you can look at the seeds of disaster from a new perspective and view them as the seeds for life renewal.

It is most often in our darkest moments that we meet our fate. If you seek within, you can find the reason for those dark moments.

What can you become as a result
of your darkest hour?

Who can you help as a result of your personal tragedy?

When will you begin to realize that *you matter*, you have value, and you are *needed* on this Earth. You would not be reading this book if this message was not meant to awaken your heart, to cause you to realize that you matter.

Individual growth is a *conscious choice*. You must take what you have, and

*Begin exactly where you are at this very moment to move
solely in the direction of the life you want to have and the
you you want to become.*

The reason you desire this life and yearn to become all you
dream you can be is that it is the *real* you, the you beneath the fa-
cade of the robotic life you have been living until now, beneath your
false perceptions and your limited views of self. Begin to see any
shred of goodness in yourself and validate it. Begin to acknowledge
any good you can possibly find in yourself that aligns with the ideal
person you envision yourself to be. Consider this: Even a thief has a
shred of goodness – he is quick. I do not condone stealing. I merely
use this as an example to show you that every human being has
traits that can be turned toward a positive purpose.

Here are the three steps you must follow to begin to take personal responsibility: First, believe that when you picture something in your mind, you can achieve it. Believe that when you
follow that "still small voice within" – your gut instinct, intuition,
or sudden idea that feels exciting, despite society's logical judgment – you will get exactly what you picture. The key element
here is to *feel* thrilled about what you picture, as if there is a guar-
antee it is on its way to you.

Second, picture your life, your *ideal* life, the work that will fill
your days with passion, and you will discover exactly what it is
you love to do. Is there a person with whom you strongly identify?
Someone who inspires a feeling inside you that speaks to your
soul? If that feeling says, "*This* is what I wish I could do!" then you
have an important clue to your life purpose.

Third, leave that horrible job, that degrading spouse, that miserable situation, and just start over again, for you! Move precisely
in the direction of the ideal life you picture in your mind. The excitement of beginning the life journey you were born to travel
will keep your courage strong whenever fear starts to set in. Each
day, you will feel excited as you begin to create the changes
needed to match the *real* you, from the inside out.

You will find that as you take personal responsibility for your life, everything you need is suddenly there for you. That phenomenon is behind the saying, "When something is right, everything just falls into place." I assure you that fulfilling your highest vision and becoming the best you can be is right, no matter who tells you otherwise.

You are not here on this earth to be oppressed, nor are you here to oppress others.

Perhaps you are in a position of authority. Would you like to have *yourself* for a boss, a spouse, or a parent? Would you want to be treated the way you treat your employees? Your spouse? Your children? What behavior would you change to turn yourself into the kind of boss, spouse, or parent you would like to have? Do it. Just because you have a habit or pattern of behavior does not mean you can't change it or replace it with a more evolved habit or pattern. You have a choice. Choose to change. You choose the words that come out of your mouth and the manner in which you say them. You choose the debilitating patterns in your life. Instead, you can actively choose patterns that will elevate you above the negative spiral of personal decay.

You choose who you will listen to when you seek advice. Once you have this advice, you must choose whether it is truly in your best interest to follow all, none, or part of it.

DISCOVERING YOUR INDIVIDUAL VALUE

Your personal power begins with the dawn
of your realization of your personal worth.

Think of yourself as a baby, as you were when you were nine months old. When you were small, your views of self were not tainted by the false words and perceptions of others.

You were pure, whole, complete.

Then, you looked at everything, saw everything, and believed in everything *other* than yourself.

You can't believe in yourself when you don't believe you are worth spending your days passionately absorbed in joyful work.

Survival, yes. We must all survive, but we are also entitled to survive with personal dignity and with joy.

We can work and love our job. We can eat and love the food. We can sleep and adore the person beside us. We can dream and see ourselves where we will one day be, if only we *decide* it is to be so.

The moment that decision is made,
your entire life does an about face, a forward march,
and you are flying toward your goals.
Yet your goals are themselves the process *during the jour-*
ney, and not *the end result.*
It is the love of the work
that brings you pleasure,
not the moment the workday is over.

How, I ask you, do you suppose you can be an effective, thriving individual if your esteem bank is empty? You can't. Your value feeds on itself, derives its pleasures and inspiration from within, from your purpose, and from the joy you receive by living that purpose.

A vast majority of the masses inhabiting Earth at this time live like robots. They are on automatic pilot, numb to their true joy.

Yet there are souls who thrive, who shine, who glow – rich in self-esteem, wealthy in self-belief, prosperous in love, and compassionately giving.

These are the people who inspire you.

Why aren't you one of them? You will become one of them the moment you *decide* to be the best you can be – because you will have taken the step to honor your worth.

To sacrifice your core self for someone else's benefit, to throw away your life to satisfy another is the biggest crime. When you do that, you steal from your very self.

And your age is not an excuse. If you believe the lie that it is too late to start over, you will regret it later. No matter how old you are, even if you are in your seventies or eighties, you are not too old to begin taking personal responsibility and creating positive change in your life.

Today is the day to begin, or tomorrow, to rise with the sun and decide *exactly who you are,* who you wish to become, and declare to yourself that you *no longer choose* to sacrifice your being, and value for the benefit of another at the expense of your very life.

When you do not take the initiative to be who you came into this life to be, then each day you face misery. And, ultimately, you will face illness because your system will be toxic from self-hate and lack of joy. It will begin to shut down because it will have nothing left to fight for.

Give yourself everything, every joy to fight for, and you will find vitality and health, and you will glow once again when you look in the mirror.

By choosing to pursue joy, you will accomplish far more than you ever could by toiling away for endless hours in a dead-end job, with personal decay as your weekly payment.

No other person is responsible for your life. When you blame another, you do not validate your true self.

If you truly want a better life,
take your life into your own hands
and create it for your very own self.

What others have does not matter. What matters is who you *are.* Once you decide who you are, you *will* become that person eventually. One moment at a time, your life will be renewed.

Take the initiative to dismantle every part of your life that causes you misery. Leave behind each task, obligation, job, person, or pattern you no longer want. Replace them with the qualities and purpose you have always dreamed of. Replace them, perhaps, with enjoying peaceful, quiet time alone or spending more time with people you care about or engaging in activities that bring you pleasure. Clean out the clutter, doubt, and negativity in your mind, and eliminate the false views so you can truly live again. You can do this easily by seeking to find the gift in any seemingly negative circumstance. Replace every complaint with a new creation. Replace every quality you feel unhappy about with the belief that you have within you the ability to be all you were born to be.

Live. See. Do. Discover. Be you! Get to know who you really are. This is your responsibility to yourself. All else follows. For how can you be there for others when you disregard your self? You can't. You need your self.

Without your self, how could you ever know the joy you will experience as soon as you decide exactly where you are going?

Begin now. You have a clean slate. The future is what you cause it to be.

Create a brand-new you, and one day you will look back and thank yourself for giving you the *gift* of you! You need permission from only one person: yourself. It's your time to thrive. The next chapter will tell you exactly how to do it.

2

HOW TO CREATE
YOUR IDEAL LIFE

*Y*our life is the result of your mental focus. Like me, you may desire a different life, a more fulfilling career, a close loving relationship, financial ease, or better health and fitness. And you deserve to experience all you desire.

If you stop to consider what's on your mind most of the time, I think you'll find that your thoughts focus on those areas of your life that you are not happy about. You probably find fault with your life and criticize yourself, when what you most certainly desire is life fulfillment and self-love.

All human beings want to feel better about themselves and their lives. People who *have* achieved self-love and who *are* fulfilling their life's passion in their work reached joy only by going through a process that was fraught with self-doubt, fear, insecurity, rejection, low self-worth, pain, and hard life lessons.

To ease your burden I will tell you that we all want the same things in life; only the form of our goals or aspirations varies from person to person.

We *all* cry. Feel insecure. Doubt. Compare. And we all worry far too much.

Perhaps you have felt some of the same things I have. I have felt petrified about not being able to pay my bills on time. I have felt sad when thinking about my career potential and realizing I was not where I knew deep inside I could actually go. I compared myself to others who were successful and wondered, "What is wrong with me? Why is my life like that of a person with a Ph.D. driving a cab?" I would look at women I admired and ask myself, "Why are *they* successful, fulfilling *their* dreams in joyful, prosperous careers, while I am struggling?" I questioned myself. I searched within. I wrote letters to God pleading for answers. And I received those answers in writing.

This book is transcribed from the answers I received. Some of the wording was so "out there," however, that I decided to put it in plain English, for you.

In our universe there is little physical proof about how to achieve the manifestation of our dream life. We have been so conditioned to live trusting just our five senses that we ignore the strongest sense of all. That sense I will refer to as instinct.

You instinctively know your potential. You feel frustrated because you sense there must be a better way. Your feelings and senses are right.

On the other hand, you are scared to death of the unlimited power and potential you have within. Your past is your comfort zone because it is the only way you know. Your unconscious negative thoughts – your complaints, worries, doubts, anxieties, fears, and insecurities – are part of that comfort zone.

But your soul, or instinct, knows all you are capable of. Your instinct trusts that you deserve and will receive what your heart truly desires.

So you have a little battle going on inside: self vs. instinct or soul.

Your heart, soul, and instinct say: "Go for it! You can do it. You were born to succeed. You deserve the best. If you want to travel to the other side of the world, you can!" So you then feel inspired or excited.

But your self steps in and says, "Are you crazy? How can you travel to the other side of the world when you don't have enough money to buy food? Be realistic. You're a dreamer. This is impossible. Stop fantasizing. Get back to reality."

Does any of this sound familiar to you? Does your heart tell you one thing and your head another?

Do you feel deep within that you are in this life for a specific purpose, and then does your logic tell you otherwise?

Do you truly believe that one person has the ability to fulfill his or her dreams, and you do not?

Do you actually buy into the lie that one person is better than you? Or do you believe that you are any better than someone else?

If you compare individual traits and qualities, or natural abilities, such as athletic ability, or intellectual gifts, then one person may have an inborn talent in one area and another person may have an inborn talent in another. Do you have a talent, gift, or inborn ability in a certain area? I would venture to say the answer is yes. Are you using it? Developing it? Exploring the possibilities or experiences you can create in your life because of it? Or, do you avoid that area altogether because it is scary to go there?

If you avoid fulfilling your inborn potential, then you avoid your life purpose. You avoid what your heart wants the most: your ideal life. This is the reason for your frustration, fear, doubt, anxiety, illness, worry, and pain.

I will give you a major indicator as to what is winning in your life: self or soul. If it *feels* good and right, it *is* right, and *that* is your heart and soul winning. That is your true essence coming to the surface. When your head jumps in and tells you every reason why what feels so right is logically so wrong, then your self has won and has pulled you back into your old comfort zone. Then you stagnate and, as a result, you feel some form of pain.

When you go with the flow of your natural abilities and desires, and follow what feels right to you, then you are moving in the direction you were born to travel. You feel excited.

When you go against your own grain because society or your head tells you that what you want is not logical or possible, then you may be living on the outside, but you feel as if you are withering on the inside.

If you are withering, that means you are not blooming. You are not being the real you. You then feel pain because you bought into the belief that living your ideal life is not safe or possible or even acceptable. To whom? Whose acceptance are you seeking? What about *self* acceptance?

You are not in this life to stagnate in your comfort zone. You are in this life to explore and experience every avenue that fills you with passion. You are in this life to *feel alive*.

How do you feel alive? Good question.

And the answer to that question is the answer to how you create your ideal life.

You do what you feel excited about doing. You love the person you feel excited with, inspired by, supported by, and accepted and understood the most by. That person is *you*.

You follow your heart, soul, conscience, and that "still small voice" within that guides you, which is your instinct. You form a picture in your mind of your ideal life, and when you feel excited, you keep reinforcing that excitement with the assurance that you *can* be, do, and have all you picture.

As soon as you feel out of your comfort zone, expect that your head will jump in with every doubt, disbelief, criticism, negative view, impossibility, and impracticality to pull you right back into the old version of yourself and your life that you are now striving to outgrow.

Suppose, for example, you are a flower seed. If you live beneath the soil, your natural life path would be to push out, explore, and dare to reach above the level of soil and bloom in the sunlight you were born to bloom in. You, as a flower seed, were not created to exist, wither, and die beneath the soil. You were created to bloom, expand, and touch the lives of others. The soil is akin to your head. It only knows darkness, the past, fears, and doubt. Your head scares you into believing that it is impossible for a tiny seed to push out from beneath inches of dirt, pebbles, and weeds, and actually flower among giant trees. But, in reality, you are the giant tree, just striving to get above ground. And, in this life, you really are, right now, everything you wish to become. But the dirt in your mind tries to keep you down.

Your mind is filled with the lies and disbelief you have bought in to.

Let me ask you a simple question. Does one flower seed have more potential to reach above ground than another?

No.

Does another human being have more potential to bloom, shine, thrive, and flourish than you do?

No.

What is the magic ingredient? I will tell you.

It is your will. Your decision. Your desire to push through the dark dirt, acknowledge its existence, and then say: "I know there is a better way. I know I was born to thrive. I know what I want, and I am going to create it by focusing on it and believing that if what I focus on feels right to me, then it is right for me.

Empower yourself with excitement. The more excited you feel, the stronger you will become. The stronger you are, the easier it will be to push through the soil of doubt and fear.

You learn lessons in the soil. You learn, as I have learned, that nothing can ever hold you back except you. When you make a decision to move your life in the direction you want most, you will feel excited. Once you feel that excitement, nothing can stand in your way. You will bloom because you are willing yourself to bloom. You will fulfill your destiny by living your purpose. Creating your ideal life is your purpose. See it in your mind, and feel it in your heart. Then you will feel alive, because you will be alive.

Without getting into a scientific discussion of how the process works, I can only tell you that it does. (And yes, there is scientific proof, which I will describe elsewhere.) The secret is in feeling excitement about what your mind focuses on.

USING THE ENORMOUS POWER OF YOUR THOUGHTS

"As you think, so you shall have."

That saying is true. But another saying, "Seeing is believing," is not – as least not when it comes to creating the life you want. For that purpose, you must turn the saying around: "Believing is seeing."

You have to picture it – whatever "it" is – mentally.

Only then will you receive it.

When you picture your ideal life, day in and day out, somehow your subconscious mind cannot distinguish between past and future. It focuses on the exact picture you hold in mind, the one you have the most feeling for.

Now, I actually did this in the form of a treasure map. This is an empowering and powerful tool you can use to create and manifest all that you desire in your life. The process is actually quite simple, and it's fun, too.

Take a pile of old magazines and cut out pictures of everything you want to be, do, and have. I mean, get down to business. How do you *really* want to look, feel, and be? What *exactly* do you want to own? Where *precisely* do you want to travel? How do you *really* want to spend your leisure time? What clubs and organizations do you wish to join, help, or create? What does your ideal mate look like? How do you want to contribute to the lives of others?

From the magazines, cut out the pictures and words that will form a large, detailed picture of your life. Your ideal life, *your dream life*. And don't hold back. Go all the way!

When I did this, I was a student in school, broke and struggling, but very excited about creating a brand-new life for myself.

One of the pictures I cut out was of the Dome of the Rock in Jerusalem. I had always wanted to go to the Middle East. I thought it would take many years for me to get there. *Six weeks after creating my treasure map, I was standing in front of the Dome of the Rock in Jerusalem.*

That was the picture that I had the most feeling for, so that was what I manifested first.

The treasure map works! The universe is not void. Our thoughts do have power.

That which we focus on, we draw directly to us.

Focus on poverty, and you will be broke. Focus on the Dome of the Rock, and you will be there. It is your choice.

Whatever you focus on,
combined with whatever you truly believe,
is exactly what you will receive.

You can't simply will it, like some sort of forced mind control. That won't work.

You have to genuinely believe in what you want to bring about in your life. The most important factor in the process is your feeling of excitement about what you want to see come into your life. Once you have true inner belief, conviction, and natural excitement, the key to receiving what you wish for is to let go. Let go and trust that you will receive all you desire, simply because you deserve to receive every joy you can conceive.

I do understand that letting go is the hardest part. But when you look at this treasure map, day in and day out, and you see in those pictures the ideal life you want, somehow, bit by bit, the pictures become your reality.

In my case, perhaps because so many of the pictures seemed to be out of the realm of logical possibility at the time, I did not expect to achieve my desires quickly; I was not *too attached* to having them become manifest right away. Each picture represented a genuine want, but how could I be emotionally attached or feel desperate about something like a trip to the other side of the world when I barely had money to buy groceries? Perhaps my lack of attachment kept me out of my own way.

When we hold on too tightly, we instill fear instead of the faith or belief or self-worth that needs to preside. Every one of us deserves to have it all in our lives. Why should someone else have it all and not you?

There is no reason – unless you believe or buy into the seemingly logical notion that you can't.

To change this, start with something small, something you truly want but just haven't been able to bring about yet. While you are trying to manifest something in your life, you must trust completely that what is meant to be yours shall in fact be yours. Place your request, from your heart, with full, *detached* conviction that – if it is meant for your highest good – you will receive what you truly desire.

Your thoughts are the seeds of your future reality.

Here's another example of how I made my thoughts become reality. As I told you earlier, after my custody battle, I completely fell apart mentally, emotionally, and financially. All I loved and cherished had been taken from me. I was at the bottom. I had no choice but to create my way up again, and this time, I had to do it on my own. Because I didn't have enough money for an apartment of my own, I rented a room in someone else's. When my roommate discovered that I smoked, she told me I had to move out. She gave me two weeks to find another place.

I was working in a clothing store and had put aside a few hundred dollars. But then I lost my job.

Now I had no job, only $300 dollars to my name, and a two-week notice to find a new place to live. This was my reality in 1998.

But I knew of this manifesting power we have in our minds, and I had an idea: I wanted to re-start a graphics business like the one I had had several years earlier. So I got my occupational license and started my own business.

For some reason, I kept picturing a Mediterranean house in my mind. That was what I had truly wanted for so long: a home with a Spanish tile roof and a garden and a bedroom for each of my children. I kept picturing this three bedroom Mediterranean house, even though I told myself, "This is ridiculous. How can I have such a house? I barely have money for gas in my car."

I visited various apartment complexes looking for a one- or two-bedroom apartment. Because my credit had fallen apart after my custody battle, I could not get approved by the leasing offices.

Then, one afternoon, that still small voice within told me, "Drive through here, in this neighborhood." Because I was starting to follow my gut instincts, I did what my instinct told me to do.

I drove through a lovely neighborhood, and there, before my eyes, was a lovely, three-bedroom, Mediterranean house, with a "For Rent" sign and a phone number. I looked at that house and, with a full heart, I said, "Oh God, I would love to live in this house." I called the phone number and met with the owner. He did not ask for a credit check, only a deposit. I gave him what I had and told him I would give him the rest the following week. I then earned the money that was required and, two weeks later, I moved into that house.

The point is that the whole time I was mentally picturing a three-bedroom Mediterranean house and truly wanting it, the logical part of my brain, the part that had been trained by society, was telling me, "This is ridiculous. Be realistic. You can't have this now."

Yet the universe gave me what I pictured mentally – gave me that which fully aligned with what I truly wanted. Instead of finding a small apartment, I was able to manifest the joy of the house I really wanted.

I had nothing, but I had everything: I had the power to create, to visualize with my mind, to believe I could make it happen, to know that I could make anything happen if I truly desired it and if it was in my best interest.

Like you, I am human, made of flesh and blood, heart and soul. I have seen the best of life, and I have had more days than I care to remember when I did not ever want to wake up again.

I have experienced the height of joy and the depths and despair of hell right here on Earth. I am no different from you. And I want to share with you my knowledge of the power of manifestation.

With patience, you can use that power to have what you want too.

Your mind wants it all *now*, regardless of whether your highest and best interest will be served in the long run. You may not see a broader perspective. Out of self-hate, you may trick yourself into worry, anxiety, doubt, agony, and pain. True wisdom about yourself does not come from your mind. Your fears about the future, however, do.

When you plant a tomato seed, you trust that you are going to have tomatoes. You do not stand over your crop counting the minutes until the harvest. You do not cry, agonize, worry, plead, wonder, beg, doubt, or fight with the soil. And you do not know all of the minute intricacies involved in the exact process of how the soil and the seed are producing a tomato plant. You just put the seed in the ground, water, and go.

The same trust must govern your intentions for what you desire to bring forth in your life. You do not need to know exactly *how* it will come about; all that matters is that it does. You – and no other person – create all that you observe in your physical reality, solely and completely. And when you buy into the false belief that another has created the misery or joy of your circumstance, then you empower that other person and thus rob yourself of your own individual power.

You allowed this other person or circumstance into your life, regardless of whether it brought you joy or pain. To claim your authentic individual power, you must stop blaming others for where you sit now, be it good or bad.

When you want to create something new in your life, the only thing that matters is your intention. If you intend for it to be so, then it is so! Just place your request exactly as you would a food delivery, and trust that it is on its way to you. Sometimes it does take longer than expected; yet be grateful for delays because delays do prove to be beneficial, and they always work out in your best interest.

STAYING IN CHARGE

If you do not take personal responsibility to actively create your future, who do you suppose is going to do it for you? No one. You create every time you think Why create unconsciously or semi-consciously when you can be the conscious designer of your life? As I've said before, no other being is responsible for your reality. It is solely and completely within *your* control. Your reality is created by *your* thoughts. That which you focus on, you do draw into your life.

If you realized the power of your thoughts,
you would probably be more conscious
of what your attention is focused on.

When you buy a new home, wouldn't you prefer to pick out, actively *choose* your carpet, tiles, paint color, curtains, door stains, appliances, and so forth? Why put more value on your refrigerator or washing machine than on your life? Don't you think you deserve to choose the design of your own life?

Yes, you do! Chose how to spend your day. Decide on your ideal job, lover, friend, career, hobby, vacation spot, everything. Create it! Actively choose it. Don't be passive.

When you allow your thoughts to be overrun by your fears, you create a fearful reality. But, when you choose your thoughts, and when you replace fearful or fear-based thoughts with positive life-enhancing thoughts, then you create a life-enhancing reality.

You *do* create your life anyway. Wouldn't you derive more pleasure from exerting conscious control over what and who come into your life?

Remember: It is your choice. You can choose anything your mind can conceive. Once you do it a few times, and actually manifest exactly what you pictured, you will realize that this is true.

LEARNING TO TRUST YOURSELF

One of the most important things in creating your future is your ability to let go, to trust, to know with absolute certainty that it is already yours. If it is within your heart, if it is in your best interest, it is true for you.

Trust your own thoughts, intelligence, and instincts rather than turning constantly to others for their permission, approval, or validation. When you are true to yourself, you will experience a strong gut feeling to move in a certain direction to manifest exactly what you seek.

When you trust yourself and go with the flow, you can follow your *own* wisdom. You are far wiser than you give yourself credit for. Authentically empowered people trust their own selves. They are secure from within and therefore are their own best friend. When you trust yourself, you have a clear mind; you can listen to your own wisdom, which will always feel right to you.

People who have been following their gut instinct and perception for a long time find that it is no longer a "still small voice" or a subtle feeling but a strong and powerful certainty.

Your certainty may run completely contrary to what others tell you is for your own good. But you will always know the truth when you listen to yourself.

You will always know, deep down inside, if something or someone is right for you or not. As long as you are true to yourself, nothing else matters. For you are the only one living your life. And the moment you stop allowing everyone else to live your life for you is the moment you will awaken to a whole new level of your brilliance.

People who are afraid to take genuine risks with their own lives tell you what you "should" do, based on what they are doing or on what they think is best for you.

Here is a simple formula to follow:

Seek advice only from those
whose shoes you would love
to see yourself in.

If there is an inspiring, empowered person from whom you can learn, then do so. But never seek approval from those whose lives you do not admire and would never want to live. To allow their comments to hinder your direction is to stifle your own inherent genius.

That sudden flash of inspiration or sudden brilliant idea is your highest knowledge; it comes from deep within the core of your being to point you in the right direction. It comes from your highest wisdom, the wisdom of your soul, the wisdom that knows how to point you in the direction you seek to go. It is my personal belief that this wisdom, sudden idea, or gut instinct comes from God. You do not have to believe in God, however; but you do have to believe in your own truth. If you get a strong, instinctive, gut feeling that tells you something, whether it is logical or not, then

Follow that hunch, that sudden idea or gut instinct.

Follow your own thoughts, feel inspired by your own vision of your ideal life, and live the reality you have always dreamed of.

In many ways, society has guided you in the opposite direction of your truest self. You "think" you are supposed to simply have a job, receive a paycheck, and struggle through the work week for the joy of your weekend.

Those in positions of authority and power do not usually guide you to find your own joy by creating your own business using your talents, abilities, and joys. If you did that, you would no longer be available to work for meager wages under their dictates, making grand profits possible for them.

It does not matter what you have done in the past or what your work is now. You may be a factory worker but wish you were an author. Pick up a pen and start writing. You may be an engineer designing water treatment facilities but what you truly want to design is a science museum for children. Do not give up your dreams for "security." This is not passionately living the life you were born to live. This is living a life you think you are supposed to live. Would you rather greet each new day with exhaustion or with passion and excitement?

The kind of life you lead is your choice. You can begin to pursue your ideal life while working in your current job. You can slowly phase out of your old life and into your new one. I had to learn to drop every activity, obligation, and person who stood in my way or was unsupportive. I refused to listen to others' negative, life-draining, logical comments. I simply pictured in my mind the result, the place I wanted to be in five years: where I wanted to live, how I wanted to look, the difference I was going to make, the places I would travel to with my children, the conferences I was going to create, the specific people I was going to invite to those conferences, and the expressions of gratitude from those whose lives I had touched.

The simple fact that you are holding this book, that you are feeling inspired to claim your own authentic individual power, and that you are, in fact, going to begin to create a picture in your mind of your ideal life – that fact is a great part of my own ideal life picture coming true. First I pictured the result; then I pursued it.

Years ago, I bought a cassette tape of a minister's sermon about creating what you want to manifest in your life. He named seven steps that stuck in my mind, and I want to pass them on to you: decide, be willing, commit, let go, follow, wait, and have.

Make a decision about everything you want, and form that mental picture. You will feel excited. Be willing to do whatever it takes, within dignity, to follow your vision. Commit fully to your vision. This is a no-holes-barred commitment to your self. Once you are fully committed to your process, you then let go. You trust that if it feels right to you, and you are committed to blooming, you *will* bloom and fulfill your purpose. Follow your gut instincts, your sudden ideas, whether they make sense to you or not. All of a sudden you may get an idea, as I have, or a gut feeling to "go into this store." It may not make sense to you. Follow it anyway. In that store may be the person who will give you the exact information you need to fulfill what you are trying to achieve. The next step is to wait. Be patient and have an accepting – and even grateful – feeling for delays. There are things to learn and people you may meet during your "delay" who will enhance your goals far better than if you had it all now. Then, after this process is complete, have it all, and enjoy it all!

As you go through this process, you become an example for others to follow. This means you also set an example for your children. In order to create their own ideal lives, your children need more than media role models and virtual reality games.

STOPPING YOUR CHILDREN FROM FOLLOWING THE CROWD

The electronic media deadens the senses, producing a hypnotized generation that exists in a world of virtual reality. Our children would be far better off if they were taught how to create their own reality and how to discover their innate gifts via interactive association with mentors and peers in clubs and organizations. Communication and relationship skills are vital

When our children go online, it would be helpful for them to discover what they would *like* to discover rather than simply chat and follow the crowd.

Adults need to listen to children to find out what they are interested in, what would they like to discover and develop and contribute. Parents and teachers should be made responsible for teaching children the skills they need to enhance their lives and become empowered. Only then will they be able to depend on themselves and create their ideal lives as they grow older. Only then will our children not be stuck in dead-end jobs, with dead-end lives, thinking they have to struggle for their security.

Society focuses on school grades, yet school shootings are becoming commonplace. Perhaps young people today are crying out for attention to their souls, their life purpose. Perhaps they're tired of virtual games that numb their minds, parents who pack their schedules with "in" activities, and overcrowded schools too stuck in the lessons of the past to take an active interest in the future of the children they teach.

Why do you think kids numb their feelings with drugs? Because they do not feel *honored and accepted* for who they really are. Instead, they are programmed by society to follow the crowd, to be whatever will draw the largest bank account. Rarely do parents say to their children, "Follow your dreams, and don't worry about the money; your happiness is most important."

Yet, how do you suppose today's children will be able to run tomorrow's world if they are caught in a virtual reality?

Their hearts and minds must be exposed to their true and passionate joys – those things they really love. When they find the joy in their own lives, only then will they be able to create a society in which personal joy and one's job or career are synonymous, a society in which work schedules revolve around family life and children never need to be home alone.

To create the best future for yourself and your children, consider your ideal life as a whole. Your car is not your life; it is simply a means of getting from point A to point B. Your dream home is not your life; it is just your shelter. And your job is not your life unless it is your daily joy that allows you to passionately fulfill your life purpose and also happens to bring you the funds you need. Your life is the daily expression of your joys, both large and small. It is the expression of your contributions to yourself, your family, society, and humanity. It is also the compassionate sharing of the lessons you learned from your pain.

Also, your future does not begin and end with you. You must consider the needs of those who are not yet in a position to create their own future, such as youngsters caught in the foster care system or those in homeless families. Reach out, teach by example, and share your success with those whose lives you come across. Share your process, your victories, your defeats, and the lessons you have learned from them all.

Our society will flourish if people take charge of their own lives and create their work, careers, values, education, and future based solely on what is in the highest and best interest of themselves and their young people.

Share your process with your children. Show them how you go about creating your ideal life. Remain open so that your children will come to you for guidance.

Do not judge them or put yourself above them. If you are harsh and judgmental toward your children, chances are great that your life is not truly fulfilled. Chances are even greater that you are caught in the trap of material validation of your self-worth, that you are not living your real life purpose, and that you are stuck in a mundane schedule of a so-called life.

The cost of education should be a top priority in society, yet, as we all see, a business would rather spend fifty thousand dollars for a full-page ad in a widely distributed Sunday newspaper than donate the money to a school in need of new equipment and supplies.

What, you may ask, does this have to do with creating your future?

When you look for ways to serve others, you will feel more of your own worth. When you realize that a great part of your purpose touches other lives, both near and far, you will realize that you are an integral part of the big picture.

When everything does not revolve around material gain, something of lasting value will come to you as a result of reaching out from your heart. When you are committed to fulfilling your ideal life, you will naturally be a role model for others.

Today's children need more role models who can show them that the joy in life comes from being and sharing, not from racing to acquire material goods.

Do you want your children to feel that their choices are limited? Only through education will they learn the skills they will need to be successful. Only through meaningful interaction with caring others will they develop the compassion, cooperation, and feelings of self-worth they need to create their own unlimited future.

If you took a more active role in creating your own future, you would naturally be so excited and happy about your creation that you might be able to offer work to others and thus create a win-win situation of self-employment that represents self-empowerment rather than selfish gain.

Today's children are rewarded with trophies. Tomorrow's children will be rewarded with fulfilled dreams.

To seek within yourself, to rely solely on yourself for the manifestation of personal joy is to create your future every day of your life. Joy is not the goal; it is the process that is rich with experience, growth, pleasure, and positive rewards for all.

TOUCHING OTHER LIVES

What part does the environment play in your future? What about our country's foreign policy? Does space exploration come into play? And what about finding space here on Earth for all the homeless people who need permanent shelter?

Many changes must take place to improve the future. What strikes a chord within you? What role will you play in the larger scheme of things? Or are you just concerned with your wardrobe, jewelry, car, vacation spot, and investment property?

If each one of us understood that our life purpose affects the future of so many others in this world, Earth would be an entirely different planet within a year.

How does your future correspond to the greater good of all?

Do you even care?

What gifts can you bring to humanity while you strive to fulfill your dreams?

Or is it solely about you?

Do you consider the potential impact of your life on those around you, or do you think your life is so meaningless that you are not capable of having any impact?

You don't have to feed the hungry or house the homeless to have an impact. You can do scientific research or floral design, nursing or manicuring. No matter what brings you joy, the process of your life can affect others.

Moreover, you do not live on this planet alone. Your future affects those around you, and vice versa. You may write a poem or create a greeting card that prevents a couple from breaking up – because your heart is in your work.

You may invent an electronic device that signals an approaching heart attack and saves lives – because you find joy in your research. You may donate a computer to a single mom who starts a home-based business that, years later, provides a fabulous opportunity to your own grandchild.

This is known as the ripple effect.

Your words and deeds cause a ripple, a wave that can potentially touch all of humanity. Your impact on one special child might be so great and so positive that he or she might grow up to prevent a world war – because of your compassion, diplomacy, caring, or generosity. The joy you feel while you express your life purpose may cause you to interact with a stranger who is contemplating suicide; that person may then decide, because of *you*, that perhaps this world is not so bad after all.

This actually happened to me. I gave work to an artist who was going to commit suicide. I gave him the work because he had talent, and he deserved to live to express his talent in his work rather than die believing he was worthless. I *know* what it feels like to feel worthless. I *have* contemplated suicide. I have been there, and it was during my darkest moments that I decided to re-create my entire life from scratch, beginning with a picture in my mind of how I wanted my ideal life to look and how I would make a difference for so many others who had lost perception of their own purpose.

When you create your future, consider the ripple effect. Think about how your actions might affect others.

Remember that money is not your goal. Bringing out your true essence, being your best self, and contributing to humanity by living your joy – that is what creating your future means. The cycle of life carries with it astounding transformations; they pave the way for you to recognize that the source of your joy is to be found within.

The source for life renewal is to be found within. The human spirit can be triumphant; men and women are able to beat the odds and succeed despite overwhelming adversity.

Far too many people are caught in a spiral of negativity. The essence of their life is drained by their robotic existence in which joy has become a foreign concept and money has become the central focus.

But for a successful future, the focus cannot remain solely on ourselves.

How tragic when a mother cannot afford to buy food for her children or a family cannot afford housing and no community program exists through which corporations can donate a portion of their profits to help those in need.

How can the focus shift from me, me, me?

It starts with you.

You can do your part by shifting the focus within your heart and mind. You can set the tone so that your voice will ring in the ears of those who have fallen deaf to the cries of people languishing in poverty and oppression.

You can start a program, a foundation, a cause, a campaign, a fight for a new law, a new paradigm for society. Or create a new bumper sticker or a new saying. What matters is your good intention, not the vehicle through which you manifest it.

Begin to create your future today. Begin with joyful contemplation on what truly matters to you in your heart, how you want to strive in your process, and whose lives you can touch with your joy.

Seek to share your wisdom, and do not contemplate or fear competition. Who else could ever be you? Call on your courage to bring out your own voice, and speak loudly yet calmly; preserve the dignity of your human spirit while declaring your right to enjoy your essence. Create your future within your thoughts and intentions today.

Release fear. Know and trust that you are here to make a difference, however small or large. Remember the ripple effect: What you do can have a profound and lasting effect on the course of someone else's life.

Cherish every moment in your day,
and as you create tomorrow,
Remember where you came from
So you never again return to yesterday.

3

SOLVING THE MYSTERY OF THE OPPOSITE SEX

*T*hrough the ages, love has both fascinated and tormented the human heart; nothing in existence feels so sublime yet gives so much pain as love. Why must there be such disparity between the two genders? Why, after so many eons, can humans race to the moon yet fail to communicate with their lovers?

The answers to this profound mystery are profound in their simplicity.

The answers are so simple that they do not register amid all the clamor of our modern world – technological advances, stock quotes, news headlines – or even amid the rote recitation of wedding vows spoken by so many couples.

THE IMPORTANCE OF TRUTH BETWEEN A MAN AND A WOMAN

People who play games in their relationships, either out of fear or to manipulate their partners, do not deal truthfully. As a result, most of those people cannot sustain their relationships for a lifetime.

For a relationship to last, it must be built on truth.

Truth must be the foundation, the structure, the cornerstone of the relationship, and the highest ideal both partners strive to attain within that relationship. Who would choose to continue in any relationship based on falsehood?

Where does this falsehood come from?
It comes from within. From within you.

It does not matter if you are male or female, young or old. What I say on these pages is truth, and from these pages the light of your being, of your soul, shall glimpse the truth of these words; and with a deep hope, you will use these words to incorporate truth into your life. Then you may indeed have and honor the truthful relationship you deserve with another.

First, there is self-truth. The truth I speak of here is what feels right inside you. You must show the strength of character and the courage to speak your truth appropriately. Whether it is understood is not your responsibility.

Your only responsibility is to be true to yourself, to validate and appreciate your own self.

If the other person does not reciprocate with truth, then the relationship is one-sided and false.

WHEN ABUSE IS CONFUSED WITH LOVE

Let me speak of abuse. Verbal abuse, name calling, and degradation. Those snide, sarcastic remarks that chip away at your self-esteem day in and day out to the point that you don't even realize it is happening anymore. But your heart does.

Let me speak of mental abuse. Mind manipulation, deceit, and game playing. Those malicious games intended to push your buttons; to hurt your feelings; to cause you to feel jealous, scared, worried, or upset.

Let me speak of physical abuse. From shoving, pushing, smacking, hitting, burning, beating, punching, or kicking to downright mutilating or even killing.

Is this love?

When you experience verbal or mental or physical abuse, is this the way love is meant to feel?

How could you possibly know true love if you buy into the belief that you have it in an abusive relationship? And, if you believe that, how could you conceive of love in any other way? If you think verbal, mental, or physical abuse is normal in a loving relationship, then you must believe you are lucky to have at least a few good days, so you better stay with it, right?

Know one thing: when you love yourself, wholly and completely, abuse does not fit in your paradigm of love. When you love yourself, you know you do not deserve any form of abuse from anyone, ever. At the first sign of abuse, you would simply walk. You would not stick around hoping it doesn't come back, because it surely will.

MARITAL ABUSE

Victims of spousal abuse have not yet learned that they deserve kindness and respect. Once they have grown enough to honor their entitlement to respect and kindness, they display that growth by leaving the abusive relationship. And, in front of the divorce judge, they may thank the abusive spouse for helping them to learn to value themselves.

Of course an authentically empowered person would leave at the first sign of abuse. But many people, especially women, tolerate all kinds of abuse out of fear: fear of not being able to survive on their own; fear of not having a place to go; fear of not being able to provide for their children alone. Many fear they will be killed by their husbands if they do leave.

Hear me now, and hear me very clearly. Abuse is a horrible crime – a crime against both the abuser and the victim. While committing abuse, the abuser does not learn, grow, or evolve as a person worthy of dignity and self-respect. While suffering abuse, the victim perpetuates the abusive pattern by remaining in the home, paralyzed by fear.

If you are a victim of abuse, you must leave. Take only the clothes on your back, if that is all you can carry, and leave. You will find help. If you don't know where to find it, go to a police station, a fire station, or a house of worship. There you will find guidance. Help is always provided to victims of domestic abuse. Just ask for it.

Consider this: If you had a job, and your employer smacked you across the face every day or shoved you against the wall because he did not like the way you typed a letter, and he called you degrading names, and he threatened to kill you or members of your family if you sought employment elsewhere, and he took your car keys away so you could not drive, would you stay at this job? Of course not. Then why stay in an abusive domestic situation?

You owe yourself the opportunity for individual growth; it is your responsibility to remain in a relationship only if it supports your efforts for individual growth. As for young children, hearing or seeing their parents as abuser and victim causes them to suffer more psychological harm then they would suffer if they needed to sleep at a friend's or relative's house or in a shelter until Mom found her own place to live again.

Some people tolerate abuse because they falsely think it is the only way they can find love with another. This is not finding love. Tolerating abuse is living with pain, not love. If you are one of these people, do not fool yourself or lie to yourself any longer. This is a lie that perpetuates the abuse. Abuse, in turn, further erodes your self-esteem, which causes you to believe that you are unlovable. So you remain caught in a circle of victimhood. Leave now.

THE SURPRISING SECRET OF GETTING LOVE FROM ANOTHER

As a self-loving person, you will recognize that you cannot, ever, make someone else love you, be good to you, be your friend, or be there for you. No matter how hard you try, and especially when you try, you cannot force love, friendship, or caring from another person.

Have you ever felt someone else wanted you to love him or her? No matter what that person did or how hard he or she tried, did it work? No. It did not.

As we all know, chemistry between two people cannot be created or destroyed. Physical chemistry is either there or it is not. But the physical relationship between two people is not the same as love.

What is this perplexing phenomenon that has plagued man and woman through the centuries? What is love? Where does it come from?

It comes from being yourself. Loving yourself. Finding honor, respect, and joy in, of, and because of yourself. Love comes when you awaken your interests, passions, and joys; when you use your talents and abilities to achieve your goals; when you thrive in areas you have not yet dreamed of; when you dare to dream even more.

Love is to be your own best friend.
To need you. To depend on you,
to honor, respect, adore, obey, cherish, and love you.
That is the key!
The key is you, not the other.

If the other also loved him- or herself, there would be no insincerity, lying, manipulation, fear, jealousy, degradation, abuse, cheating, or fighting. There would be differences of opinion and differences in preference or perspective, but not war between the other and you.

There would be a sweet, magnetic chemistry. Then there would be friendship.

In this friendship between two people who love, respect, and understand themselves there would be honesty with each other. People would not hold back their real feelings because to do so would be to lie to themselves as well as to the other.

People would not stop a meaningful activity simply because someone called them for a date. The date would be set for another time.

People would not be upset or jump to melodramatic, illogical conclusions just because they have not heard from a special someone for a few days. They would hope all is fine with the other person and would trust that they will be in touch when the time is right.

People would not feel they have to be with each other simply because the calendar says it's Friday or Saturday. There would, however, be regard for each other's feelings, and both would assume that if they would like to get together, then it would be more appropriate to make tentative plans than no plans at all.

In our society, it is no secret, no surprise at all, that when two people start to date, all kinds of expectations arise; all kinds of games are brought into play. No wonder there are so many people home alone at night. Who needs the games; who wants the insincerity? Nobody!

The key word here is "want."
You have to want nothing.
You have to be everything, for you.

When you have grown and evolved enough to be your own dearest and best friend, and when you have grown and evolved enough to encourage another to do whatever he or she needs to do for happiness or fulfillment, that is when you can be sure the special person in your life will be the mirror image of you.

That person will play with you and challenge you to be your very best. That person will honor himself and understand his own perspective, feelings, beliefs, attitudes, principles, preferences, and desires. And that person will naturally love, honor, and understand you.

When you let go of all of the wanting, the longing, the desperation, the agonizing, and the fear, you find something wonderful and magical happens: you have it. You have love.

Stop trying; start being.

Stop doing everything to *get* that other person. Start being everything you want to be for you, and you will find that person will one day open his eyes and see that you are the one he's been searching for all along.

This is what it means to let go, to move on. You don't throw your love out the window; to the contrary, you throw out your focus on loving the other. And you fill that void with love of self.

When you see yourself
as the source of your own pleasure,
you do not need it
to come from another.

As this need vanishes, you become even more desirable than you would be if you were at another person's beck and call.

For how can people desire that which they have, and how can they strive to attain the level of intimacy they deserve if it is given to them so freely, so easily, without having been earned?

When you work toward a mutual, beneficial relationship, you both bring and contribute your gift of self to the union.

Whether it is for a day, a year, a decade, or a lifetime, each person contributes the very essence of himself or herself.

You each already know exactly where you stand, what behaviors you will accept, and which ones you will not put up with.

How to end a sabotaging pattern within a relationship

Whether you are in a relationship that has just begun or one that began decades ago, if you are not satisfied with the behaviors you are shown, simply change your response to those behaviors, and a reaction will result.

Your partner's reaction will have to change to reflect the changes in your attitudes, your guidelines and boundaries.

All you can change is you.
All you can control and manipulate

is your own choice.
You can react to what you are shown,
or you can leave the source of discomfort in your life.

For as you change, as you grow, your reactions do as well. You break the cycle of dysfunction within a relationship when you choose to respond in a new, more highly evolved fashion.

When you love another, your communication of self-love is what allows the love to flow between you. Not a wall, not a game, not a punishment, not lashing out, not carrying on hysterically, but only love of self communicates what you see, feel, or observe to be beyond the boundary of what you will tolerate.

When you whine, beg, plead, cry, yell, scream, throw, hit, or lash out, your actions do not deserve the respect you ultimately are entitled to.

But when you openly and calmly share anything that displeases you, anything that causes you to feel unvalued or unappreciated, then you have genuine communication. Then you have friendship, understanding, respect for each other's feelings, and the integrity to preserve the good you have found.

Build a new bridge of understanding over the turbulent waters of confusion and pain. Allow past hurts and pains to flow out of your system and out of the dynamic of your relationship by sharing truth honestly, deeply, and purely When you both do that, truth and understanding will replace chaos and pain.

MELTING THE WALLS THAT STAND BETWEEN YOU

Much of the discord couples experience comes from fear of exposing their true feelings – their love, fears, doubts, insecurities – their true selves. So they hide their truth behind ego, pride, defense mechanisms, stories, lies, and games instead of communicating authentically.

When you do this, it robs you of your own solid foundation, your feelings of strong self-worth, self-respect, and high self-esteem. When you are too afraid to expose the real you, then you play the games that destroy a genuine healthy relationship or romantic friendship. But as you heal and realize there is nothing so terrible to hide, you then begin to feel more secure to share your truth. As you do this, you reinforce your self-worth and, at the same time, you reinforce the relationship's foundation with truth.

When two people love, they have a common ground from which to build a new foundation based on trust, mutual respect, and mutual understanding. Yet, there must be compromise. One cannot yield all the time. Satisfaction of needs, wants, requests, and desires must be reciprocal.

Think about the word "relationship." Relate your concerns and feelings on the ship of your making, so you may travel together on a sea of understanding.

If you begin a relationship with a pre-set agenda, you will find that you are not being your real self. You act the way you think the other wants you to act. You toss aside many of your goals, interests, dreams, and aspirations because you think that doing so will allow you to "get" this man or this woman. And in that process you steal the foundation of your truth, of your core, from your very self, and you prevent the other from knowing your inner beauty.

Like so many people, you may try to be perfect at the beginning of a relationship. You try to look your best, act your best, feel your best. But you leave out the most important ingredient: the real you, which is the best you. Like so many people, you think that if you showed the real you, your potential partner would surely run, leaving skid marks on the way.

What is so wrong or terrible with the real you?
Perfection is not exciting. It is boring.

If you always try to be perfect, you create discomfort with the other person and actually prevent the growth of true friendship and intimacy.

Where are her moods? Doesn't he ever get angry? Does she always look so perfect? Doesn't he ever have a bad day? Why can't she show me she gets mad? Doesn't he have any real feelings? Is she always so intellectual? Does he really have a heart? Where is it? How can I show my real self if he or she doesn't do it too?

You see, when you both present your real and genuine selves to each other, you lay a solid foundation from which you can develop an honest and meaningful friendship or romance with one another.

You may know that many times people will test others to see what they will put up with, what they will tolerate. Testers want to find out how much they can get away with. They also want to know whether the testees have enough respect and regard for themselves to put the testers in their place if they cross the line.

Sometimes the one you date
wants to see that you have guts,
that you are not a spineless wimp,
that you do have self-respect,
that you will only tolerate being treated
with common decency and respect.

So, show it! If others say something to you that strikes a chord within, and you don't like the feelings you are getting as a result of their words or actions, you must speak up and say so. Now.

You can say it gently and graciously,
but make sure that it is said.

By speaking up, you honor and preserve your self-esteem, your personal dignity. Others then know how you feel as a result of what they did or said, and they know what you are requesting of them; it then becomes their choice as to whether they will honor your personal boundaries.

Each person is entitled to all of his or her own beliefs, opinions, preferences, joys, and individuality.

You do not own others; they are not your property. You share your time or your life together. As you learned in nursery school, sharing is giving; it is not taking, and it is not demanding that another does it all your way.

A WORD FOR RELATIONSHIP DICTATORS

If you try to control your partner, I ask: Who do you think you are? What gives you the right to control and manipulate your spouse or friend? Why should someone else behave the way you see fit and ignore his or her own interests and personal growth? Are you so fearful of growing on your own that you shield yourself by controlling and undermining your partner? Do you feel so unworthy of your partner that you compensate by giving orders, acting like a dictator, and instilling fear when you should be opening your heart, sharing your pain, and creating the joy you are entitled to? Instead of demanding joy from your partner, give it to yourself.

If you and your partner are stuck in a dysfunctional spiral – one of you the controller; the other, the puppet – this message is for you: Controllers always feel inadequate. The very act of attempting to control another person makes controllers feel minimized as human beings. They do not feel empowered. They hide their fear and lack of self-validation behind a wall of orders, rules, and dictates.

If you want to experience genuine control, then you musk take a risk: Open your heart, share the real truth, and knock down the wall you put up.

ENCOURAGEMENT FOR THE DOORMATS

I used to be the world's biggest doormat, so I speak from personal experience here. If you are a doormat, then you have not taken personal responsibility to actively change your life. Instead, you whine, cry, feel miserable, dance as the controller pulls your puppet strings, and choose to remain in your familiar comfort zone of misery. You don't dare to risk the unknown. You don't dare to love yourself.

You don't dare to see yourself existing and even thriving under the dictates of no one but yourself.

Perhaps you are not being controlled, but you have been stuck in a pattern of trying to get your partner to respond to your needs. Did you ever consider that you could stop trying, and fill those needs yourself?

The reason so many of us are trying so hard is that we each have a hole within, and that hole can only be filled by ourselves, which is the hardest thing to do.

Do not think that as the author of this book, I sit on a throne of relationship perfection, all whole, all together, without a shred of work to do on myself. That would be the lie of the millennium.

We learn the most from our greatest mistakes. When we try so hard to force another to be or act a certain way, and we are unsuccessful, we are left with only one choice: the mirror. Wanting to know why others treat us the way they do is like asking the mirror why it shows us our reflection.

What you see in the mirror are *your* areas of growth, not the other person's. You have a responsibility to open your eyes to *your* growth rather than to focus on the other person's.

Ask yourself, "What do I want from my partner that I am not giving to myself?" If a pattern repeats itself in your relationships, ask yourself, "What am I trying to get? What outcomes am I so attached to?" You will find that there is an area within that needs to be healed – by you.

For me, that area involved love and validation. To be perfectly loved meant that I was lovable. It was the proof I never had growing up. It was the validation I never had when I was a child.

I sought love from someone else to fill that hole within. That hole caused me to feel and act needy and clingy; it caused me to give, give, and give. I felt depleted, hurt, angry, and resentful. What I really needed most was to love and validate me, need me, and be good to me. I learned that if someone else could not do that for me, for whatever reason, it was not a reflection of my own worth.

The behavior of another never reflects your own worth. It may be, however, a genuine reflection of a part of you that lies so deep and is crying out to be healed. This healing only you can give to yourself. It can never come from another. And the more we try to get it from another, the more resistance we will encounter.

Eventually, the resistance builds to the breaking point. We pull, and tug, and demand, when all the while we need to pull back, pull within, and reach deep down to bring out what we are so afraid we can never get: love.

Beneath the veneer of status and success, so many of us just want to feel we are lovable, worthy, accepted, and valued.

The other night in my kitchen, I thought of a simple analogy. If you were a doughnut, and you sought to fill your hole with love from another doughnut, and it poured its flour into your center hole, would it ever fill it? No matter how many doughnuts (or relationships) you go through, no one can fill that hole within. No matter what others do, your hole will still be there.

But if you fill your own hole with self love, approval, validation, and joy, then you will truly enjoy what others add, because you will feel and be complete.

I admit that I just learned this. I made mistakes, had failures, and focused on another person when all the while I should have been giving to myself.

The pressure we place on others to fill that hole drives them away. It is not fair. It is not necessary, and it must change. You must change it. I had to learn to love me and give me what I kept trying so very hard to get from another.

I had to learn to recognize the pattern. And I learned that whenever I went into giving overload, pouring out my heart, giving to another with little or no return, *that* was when I needed to give to myself.

When we recognize an old, ingrained pattern,
then we take personal responsibility to change it for the better.

As we change the patterns, the negative effects they have had on our lives go away, and we heal.

As the inner pain goes away, we feel peace. That is what I feel when I heal. Pure inner peace. I found my source of love and fulfillment: it lies within. It does not lie within the other. It lies within oneself.

If you have ruined a relationship due to this common pattern, take heart. If the one you love truly loves you, he or she most probably will return. Your new, authentically empowered, and genuine growth will be felt, seen, sensed, and will naturally bring what you were previously seeking from the other. The pressure will be gone. Your inner need will be gone. Then, you can have the type of relationship you want.

So, again, what do you want for yourself?

How do you prefer to feel when you are in a relationship?

If you consciously choose to create the relationship you deserve with your self, you will find that you will no longer entertain the company of those who undermine you or those who simply are not right for you. You will never settle again!

*Would you serve cookies and tea to a person
who walked through your front door
and defiled your home?
No, you would not!*

So why would you continue to serve a person who defiles you on a daily basis? A person who does not honor and respect you?

Your whole paradigm will change once you receive what you need from your inner self.

If these issues surface in one partner in a truly empowering relationship, his or her healing will naturally spark the desire for healing in the other partner. There would be no struggle. Change would be a matter of preference, not obligation. The other would either grow or not.

*We do not have any right to demand that
another grow for us.
The growth of another is not our responsibility.*

Yet, relationships bring out our greatest challenges. That's why they are so special. When we honor and respect the idea that self growth, relationship growth, and getting to the other side of those challenges requires time, patience, and dedication, we are not so inclined to throw in the towel when we encounter problems.

That is the beauty of working through the challenge: the rewards are indescribable.

Sometimes a breakup is the only way to bring about the environment we need for self-contemplation and self-realization.

A breakup is not the worst thing in the world. Sometimes, it is the darkness before the dawn: the darkness of introspection and self truth, which reveals to us our greatest mistakes, our areas most in need of healing, and our responsibility to come out of that darkness a far better person than we were before.

A breakup can be a healthy break away from the old ways into brighter days ahead.

Yes, breaking away from the old patterns is scary, and it is the fear itself that makes it difficult to move from recognizing the problems to actually doing something about them.

So, how do you start to change a negative pattern in a relationship with someone you love? Or someone you only think you love when what you really love is the security of feeling you are not all alone?

Well, either way, you begin by loving your self.

If you are married or living together, do not get caught up in the negativity of the other's dysfunction. You do not have to fight back when you are faced with negative comments. You certainly do not have an obligation to cook, do laundry, clean, or be home for this person either.

If you are barraged with undermining treatment, just do things for you. Cook for yourself only! Take yourself out to a movie at night, alone! Go out to dinner, alone, or with a friend or neighbor. And do let your negative partner know that when he or she has grown enough to display common courtesy and respect toward you, then you would be happy to do those things again.

No fighting, no hysteria, and no *you* to turn to, to fulfill their needs, when they do not treat you with the respect you are entitled to. As you take a stand for you, remain calm and peaceful.

As you grow to love you,
something wonderful happens.
Your need for the other vanishes.

If they do desire your company, then they will treat you appropriately. And then you can *choose* to be there for them again.

THE GREATEST RISK, THE SWEETEST REWARDS

To be there, to love, what is the price?

What will it cost you to receive all you are entitled to? To be in a relationship, there is a payment that must be made if you wish to receive all you desire from the other.

If your payment is fear, withholding your true feelings, holding back, allowing fear to block the flow of truth, then you receive loneliness and validate your own lack of self-worth. This validation only breeds further feelings of alienation; you do not experience all the rich joy you can receive when your payment is genuine truth.

To share your truth is perhaps one of the scariest feelings that exists between lovers and romantic friends today.

When you take the risk to bear your soul, expose the real you, and reveal your genuine feelings, you become vulnerable; you may be afraid that your open heart will be pierced by another.

But there is another dynamic you may wish to consider and experiment with, a tiny bit at a time.

Risk exposing your feelings.

Take a tiny risk, just as a baby takes a tiny risk with his first steps. Yes, your fears may cause you to stumble, to close your heart again. But if you are with a person you truly love, and you take a baby step to expose your truth, then you can see the reaction. Then you can see how you will be treated as you risk sharing the genuine feelings you hold inside.

If you are with a person you truly love, and you do take tiny steps to share your genuine feelings, you will find that you are rewarded with love, acceptance, and appreciation in return.

Then take another step, take an action, do something special together, and watch, feel, and be amazed at the new joy you will discover.

As you take tiny steps, first with vision and will, then with action, you will find the rewards are akin to those of a baby learning to walk: "Wow, I can do it!" The baby thinks, "I will do this again!"

After many attempts of risking to share genuine love and true feelings, you will find that you stumble back into old patterns far less than you did before. And you walk beside the one you love more easily. And soon you may want to run together – to dare to go all the way, to run, and laugh, and experience the true freedom and joy of sharing your true self, your true and honest feelings with the one person who has truly been there for you through all your past stumblings.

When you find this with another, you have found real love.

You have found one with whom you can share your deepest fears, your greatest insecurities, your biggest mistakes, and still be loved and appreciated for all of who you are.

When you find such a person in your life, you must know there is a reason for this to have happened to you. You may choose to take a deeper look beyond the simple romantic or friendly attraction and realize that perhaps there are greater reasons, higher reasons for your finding one another.

Perhaps you are to do something together. Perhaps you are to truly be there by each other's side, a hand to hold, arms to hug, love to feel, fun to share, friendship to grow, trust to bloom, and memories to create that you can treasure together for your life.

There have been many people who have turned their backs to the love they have found, and in each case, those people have never forgotten, nor have they ever been able to replace their true match with another. They live with regret. They live with a heart longing for the joy and beauty they once had but were too afraid to embrace fully; they turned their backs on the one they truly loved, and never found such a true love again.

Love, pure love, honest and genuine love, does not die.

You can travel to every corner of the globe. You can watch the seasons pass. But no matter how far you travel or how many years have gone by since you held the one you love in your arms, your heart, your soul will never forget this one person.

You may also find that the one who brings out your greatest growth, who makes you see all of the areas that need healing is precisely the person you may find yourself wanting to run away from. Who wants to face all of that hurt? If that happens, be wise enough to ask yourself, "Isn't that why we have true relationships, to genuinely become the best we can be?"

And how can we become our best when we ignore or run away from those areas we need to heal? We cannot.

So the one who causes you great frustration is also the one who ultimately brings you the greatest joy: the discovery of the genuine you.

Once you do grow through the challenges, the rewards of such a deep and genuine understanding between two people could never be replaced by a shallow, superficial relationship.

Love is a gift, and appreciation for this gift must be shown. There is the saying, "Hurt me once, shame on you; hurt me twice, shame on me." This universe will send you a gift of love, a true match, once. If you choose to throw this gift away, if you do not show appreciation for it, you can be certain this universe will not be foolish enough to give you a gift so rare and so special again in this life.

You must know that when a person treasures you, when he or she sees through to the core of you and accepts you fully, with all of your faults, you have been blessed.

Now, if you love this person, if you truly do, deep inside, love this person, then give yourself this gift of love, cherish and treasure the gift you have received, for if you do not, you shall not ever know such a gift again in this life.

You will know deep down in your heart when all of the elements are there. You will feel so at peace and, at the same time, so challenged – challenged to grow, challenged to evolve and lift yourself above and beyond your fears of intimacy. This work on self is required in order to continue experiencing the gift of this love in your life.

Debilitating fears of closeness or of opening one's heart are also patterns that must be recognized and worked through. So ask yourself, "How can I notice when those old feelings come up?"

Become conscious of them. If you remain on automatic pilot, you will automatically sabotage the relationship.

Fear of being hurt or vulnerable is understandable and quite common. When left unnoticed, unchecked, and unattended to, however, it is also the source of pain. How do you attend to your fears? You simply acknowledge their existence. You say, "Oh look, this is what I have been feeling, this is what happens to me. Do I want this feeling or pattern to take charge, or do I prefer something different?"

It comes down to a preference, an individual choice not to react but to consciously decide how you are going to respond when you notice your fears coming to the surface. Once you become fully conscious of them, their paralyzing effect dwindles; instead of feeling smothered by an avalanche, you feel the slight sting of a pebble. Awareness of an old pattern greatly reduces its effects on you.

There is always a period of tremendous anxiety when old fears come to the surface. Realize, however, that this anxiety does, in fact, pass. It is a feeling. Feelings flow. One feeling, no matter how horrible or anxiety provoking, does not last forever.

So once you notice the anxiety coming to the surface, you become the one in charge. You are no longer run by old tapes that do not help you experience all you prefer to experience now.

Those old tapes may have served you in the past, protecting you from pain from a certain person. But now that you have found someone else, someone special, those old tapes can only be destructive.

If you become aware of your feelings and allow the anxiety to pass by sharing what you think and how you feel, then you no longer risk losing a person you may not ever be able to replace.

This is far better than allowing old, self-protective patterns that are in your comfort zone to destroy your opportunity for genuine love and genuine healing. Would you rather lose true love because it feels uncomfortable?

Is that what you want?

Look around you. Think of all the people you have dated. Think of how many years you have gone without this one very special person. Do you want to lose this gift simply because it is scary for you to take personal responsibility and notice your feelings as they surface?

You do not have to be perfect. You cannot be perfect. But if you decide to take charge of an old pattern and act to heal your inner self, you will find that the one you love will not leave your side.

THE PERFECTION FALLACY

One thing is certain:

When two people love, love truly, love deeply,
they will make mistakes.

They will walk and then stumble. They will walk in love and stumble from fear. But you can be certain that as long as you get up and decide to walk again, the one you love will always be there for you, after you stumble, after you decide to walk again.

You cannot ever lose a true love when you make mistakes, when you stumble, when you temporarily return to some old pattern you are seeking to replace with healthier new ones.

So go ahead: walk, stumble, and look up. You will see the one who truly loves you is still there, waiting to walk beside you again, so you may one day run in laughter and pleasure together.

It is a complete fallacy to believe
that perfect love means perfection.

Here is the truth:
Perfect love means growing from and learning from imperfection, recognizing your mistakes, and becoming your best. This is what relationships are all about:

Sharing your life with the one you love,
the one who loves you in spite of your mistakes,
the one who expects you to grow and learn,
stumble, and walk again, by their side.

We grow in love and in relationships through our mistakes. We do not grow in isolation or in theory.

We grow from hard experience: making mistakes, hurting, regretting, crying, realizing, making new choices, healing, and showing our new growth. We can do that only in relationships. They are sacred ground because of their astounding effects on our personal growth.

You will discover that the word "forgiveness" is the balm that soothes the scrapes after you stumble with every mistake you make.

"Forgive" means "to you, for you, I give my love, no matter how many times you may stumble."

That love is the gift for you, given for you when you risk taking personal responsibility to acknowledge your mistakes, your fears, and your failure to live up to your very best.

Mistakes are most commonly made when your fear of opening your true heart becomes stronger than your need to share your love. Or when you try so hard to get love from another and you behave in such a needy, clingy fashion that you drive the other away – because you have not yet learned how to genuinely give love to yourself.

So, what happens? You lose the one you love, you throw or push him away. But, because true love never dies, you realize your loss; and the pain and the regret you feel swells up inside of you casting out fear, replacing it with the truth of your love. Now you want your love back, so you are ready to show your true feelings; you are willing to show the real, empowered you.

That is why so many love songs are written about wanting your real love back, about being reunited with your true love. Real love cannot ever die. It certainly cannot be killed by space, time, distance, or fear. It also cannot die when you stumble.

So as your desire for your true love swells up inside, you want your love back. This is a dangerous game to play. Sometimes your love will reunite with you, forgive you, and be there for you, but there is a limit. There is a limit to how much one is willing to go back to the old ways. So if you don't work hard to replace old patterns with new ones, you risk losing this real love forever.

There is only one way to avoid that loss: Grow. Learn from your past errors. Learn and grow beyond the restrictions of ego and beyond the doubts of self-worth. Give to your self, give for you! And as you do this, the other will forgive you.

Give, and you shall receive.

If your love is pure, if your lessons have been acknowledged, if your efforts are moving in a healthy direction, you will be forgiven of your past mistakes.

Why would people waste the gift of their love on others who do not have enough self-regard to give growth to themselves?

Would you give people diamonds if every time they took them they flushed them down the toilet?

How many times would you keep reaching deep within to bring forth the diamonds of your heart and soul to give them to a person who flushes your gifts down the toilet?

So, my friend, if you have been stumbling, I do suggest you acknowledge this to yourself, first. And if you have found diamonds in one person on this Earth who you know truly loves you, then I do suggest you get up and do your best to walk again. Walk over to this person, and hold them. Give them a hug and say, "Thank you for being here for me." Say, "I am going to do my best, even if it is just a baby step at a time; I am going to do my best so I can have the best person for me in my life as my friend, as my lover. And that person is you." Do and say that if you have been withholding love.

But if you have been pouring a reservoir of love on to another, then you shine for you. Indulge in your life, your goals, your own worth, and your achievements, and dare to show how you don't *need* anymore. But it is a *gift* for another to enjoy your company. A pure gift – not in a cocky or conceited way but in a glowing way, a way glowing with self-love, self-respect, self-validation, and sheer joy.

Do you think you could ever lose with this approach?

For when someone truly loves you, they know that they too have stumbled in the past, they too were once filled with regret from making mistakes, and they too came to you and acknowledged where they went wrong. And you forgave them and walked hand in hand.

So go, walk, stumble, learn, apologize, forgive, and treasure the love you have found. Don't let it go. Don't grow old with regret as your companion. Risk opening your heart, risk shining from within, and the love and inner peace you find will forever soothe your soul.

How to handle "I'm not ready to settle down yet"

How can one person's needs be met if the other is not ready to give what is required to allow a romantic relationship to evolve into a meaningful lifelong union?

If one person is ready to move forward, ready to create a more intimate connection, and the other is not, what then?

Many people could have reached the level of intimacy and commitment they desired if they had only received the patience, compassion, and understanding of the other. Yet many people are childish when it comes to matters of the heart. Many do not have the patience to work on a relationship if it does not fulfill all of their expectations as quickly as they would like. As a result, you have breakups, people longing for each other, people with pain in their hearts, when simple compassion and understanding could have brought them all they desired over time.

Many people end relationships because they do not understand that friendship is the key – that they need to build trust and enjoy the company of the other without all the formal dating or courtship behaviors.

Yes, courtship, dating, sex, romance are all vital to a romantic relationship, but there are many people who have issues of intimacy to work through first. Many people need to go slowly and build trust, reaching a certain comfort level with someone before they can commit themselves. So in this case, if one is ready for a committed, exclusive relationship and the other is not, instead of hastily and prematurely ending the relationship, turn it into a friendship.

Stop the pressures of dating and courtship. Allow yourselves to bond in a deep, respectful, and trusting union as friends, as best friends.

If the attraction is there, if the chemistry is right, if the two of you have much in common and share meaningful goals, why should that beautiful experience be ended completely? Instead, you can continue the growth and development of your friendship, which, after all, is the true foundation of any real marriage.

So if you are ready for commitment and your partner is not, release the pressure and just be friends. Best friends. No sex, no dates, no candlelight intimacy. You will find that as the bond of friendship grows, as the trust deepens, the one who was not previously ready suddenly is ready. And you have been there all along. You reached from your heart to give understanding instead of demanding a commitment of emotions and actions the other was just not ready to give. Time heals fear.

Time builds trust, and love grows over time.

You may find, however, that the physical chemistry is still strong. If you genuinely want to share love-making or passion with each other, do not deny this or suppress it, because to do so causes tension. Go with the flow of your genuine feelings. If you feel attracted to each other, show it. If you want to sleep together and hold each other, do so! There is no wrong in showing love. The wrong is to deny your love, your chemistry, and your feelings only to conform to a rigid belief or "should" with regard to society's dating or courtship expectations. There is no "should," there is only truth. If you feel love and attraction, don't withhold it; show it.

If one of you desires a monogamous relationship and the other is simply not ready for that, then you must decide what is most important to you: genuinely sharing the time you do have together or settling for not having each other in your lives at all.

When you allow the word "should" to control your life, you find that you are no longer in control of achieving all you want. This is not the same as "settling." Settling is when you deny what is genuinely in your heart because your head tells you it is wrong and that you "should" do or not do something.

Is it truly wrong to sleep with someone you adore and are physically attracted to just because you are not ready to make a formal monogamous commitment?

No.

Is it genuinely wrong to sleep with someone you care for deeply and are attracted to because it is not an exclusive, monogamous relationship?

No.

The only "should" that can appropriately govern your life is that you should do what is genuinely in your heart. No matter what society tells you, no matter what anybody tells you, if it is true and right in your heart, then it is true and right for you. That is being your own best friend as well as a best friend with the one you love but are not formally committed to.

Commit to the genuine truth in your heart. Express that, and you will feel validated, whole, and complete within.

One reason relationships fail is that one person seeks validation by the other. But when you validate your own worth, when you receive respect and admiration from yourself and do not need it to come from the other, then you will possess a quality that is the foundation of pure love: the ability to give.

To give understanding in place of expectation.
To give patience in place of haste.
To give compassion in place of ego fulfillment.
To give friendship instead of demanding a commitment
the other may not be ready to make.

For as you sow, so shall you reap. As you give, so will you be given to in return. As you reach out of your comfort zone to be there for the other, you will find that in time, they will reach out of their comfort zone to return your goodness to you.

They will give, they will commit to you, for you will have shown them that you are worthy of their commitment, and they shall ask you to share your life with them.

For it is the one who endures both the good times and the difficult times who ultimately wins the love, respect, admiration, and commitment from the other. It is very rare to have someone in your life who will be there for you as a true friend; this is a gift.

Relationships are testing grounds; they test the bond, the endurance, the respect for oneself and for the other.

How can you expect someone to make a lifelong commitment to you if they do not first see that you are capable of meeting the challenges that arise during the early stages of a relationship?

You see, life brings challenge. Life brings circumstances that you must overcome. If you love a boyfriend or girlfriend, and they cannot be there for you through the early challenges of the relationship, how can you possibly expect them to commit to you for life?

Couples who have successfully worked through the challenges of their relationship will tell you that it requires work on self and beyond the needs of self to truly be there for the other; it takes work to build a relationship that can endure the tests of life and the test of time.

WHEN YOU'RE NOT READY, BUT YOU CAN'T LET GO

Life will keep giving you the same challenge in all of your personal relationships until you face it head on and work it through.

For example, if you have a problem with commitment or intimacy, you will find that same challenge in each relationship, until one day you meet that one person who causes you to look within – to search your heart to find the answer. For when you find true love, another soul with whom you feel an indescribable bond, that person will cause you to seek within to heal the problem that blocks the flow of happiness you deserve in your life.

And when you do seek within for a solution, you will have all you truly desire. If you do not, then you shall live with regret. To seek or not to seek is always your choice.

You can choose to run from one empty relationship to another, year after year, or you can choose to realize that fulfillment comes when the bonds of love and friendship are combined, and that those bonds are far too valuable and precious to discard once you have found the one person who causes you to turn yourself around. When you have healed through that relationship, you will be ready to commit yourself to that person with true love.

UNDERSTANDING THE MOST COMMON CAUSE OF RELATIONSHIP TENSION

Men and women often feel that the opposite sex is truly from another planet. How amazing it is for both male and female to be human beings made of flesh and blood, heart and soul, yet naturally and instinctively be so different in certain areas.

One difference in particular causes much confusion and unnecessary pain.

When a woman falls in love, she wants closeness and more closeness, and she wants that closeness to permeate all levels of her life. Most women do not want or need space after they make love. They would hold the man they love all day if they could.

When a man falls in love, he too wants closeness; but then he needs space – time alone, time to regain his senses, time to bring his heart, mind, and emotions back under his control.

During the early stages of an intimate relationship, a woman may become upset and feel insecure if she does not hear from the man she loves as soon or as often as she thinks she should.

The man, on the other hand, feels content, at peace with himself, and does not necessarily feel this need to continue a state of closeness.

When a woman falls in love and is physically intimate, she wants to bake heart-shaped cookies at the very moment the man wants to play racquetball with his male friends. If the woman calls him then, he may feel smothered. He needs his personal space. This is not a rejection of the woman; it is just that men and women have different needs.

Men like closeness followed by space. Women like closeness followed by more closeness.

To solve this problem, the best thing a woman can do after a lot of intimacy is to plan an activity that will absorb her attention so she will not cling to the man. Allow a man his space, and he will keep coming back.

The best thing a man can do after intimacy is to give the woman a sweet, two-minute phone call or send her flowers to show her that he cares. Then she will not feel rejected, and he can have his time alone knowing that he's done the right thing.

What "till death do us part" really means

Let me address this issue of eternity, this promise many couples demand of each other and recite in standard wedding vows. Taken literally, this promise is broken more than it is kept. But "till death do us part" can be interpreted differently.

In this phrase, "death" does not need to mean the end of physical life. It can mean the end of the couple's purpose for being together; once the purpose is fulfilled, the union no longer needs to continue.

Now that I have just shocked and mortified the majority of the human race, please allow me to explain further so you can have a clearer and deeper understanding.

When two people meet and grow in love, the purpose of their meeting is to help each other in a certain area, on a certain level of their lives. Now, I shall go into this in more detail in Chapter 4, Soul Mates. But here, I am not speaking of soul mates; I am speaking of those couples who find themselves in divorce court even though they once promised to be together for the remainder of their lives.

Of course there is nothing wrong with traditional marriage. It is a lovely concept. With all of the single parents in society today, however, this idea of "till death do us part" needs clarification.

How could you possibly promise something about a time that is decades away? How could you possibly be so sure that you and your partner will continue to grow together for the remainder of your lives and not grow apart? Why would you promise something you might not be able to fulfill?

Two people meet for a particular reason, a reason related to emotional growth or lessons to be learned to foster that growth so that they can become all they are meant to be, become who they really are, as opposed to their false perceptions of self.

Think about your own relationships or marriages. Was there one in which you felt so in love at first? And did you discover after a while that that particular partner had provided you with an opportunity for personal growth – an opportunity to awaken those aspects that had been dormant within you? And after you grew, did you still want that same person to remain as your partner?

Judging from the statistics on divorce in this country, my guess is that about half of the people reading this would answer "no." Someone entered your life; as a result of that relationship, you grew to be more of who you really are. When the relationship fulfilled its purpose, you no longer felt the need to remain together, so you went your separate ways.

But in many cases, two people are meant to share the remainder of their lives together; those are the couples who are still happily married decades later, and this is perfectly fine as well.

So, it is not that marriage is right or wrong, good or bad. It is a wonderful thing to be with one person for as long as the relationship is of mutual benefit, to help each other grow, to explore life, to engage your minds in new areas. But to remain together because of some recited obligation, long after you do not fit into each other's life, long after you have stopped growing and have no common purpose – that is the same as signing a contract with an employer stating, "I will work here, in this job, until death do us part. And no matter how my interests or life goals change, no matter how dissatisfied I am with this job, no matter how many other areas of my life I could fulfill if I were to have a different job, I will still stay with you as long as I live."

Does this make any sense at all? Of course not! Yet that is what couples do when they promise to remain together for the remainder of their lives.

This is a ridiculous promise. In many cases it cannot and should not be fulfilled; in other cases it is wonderfully fulfilled.

Instead of promising to remain together forever, why not agree that you will be committed to each other as long as you can truly grow together, be there for each other, support each other's individual growth, be a true friend to each other, and as long as your union serves your highest good in all areas. Agree that if you grow apart, if your goals, perspectives, lifestyles, desires, purpose, interests, or intellectual and spiritual growth takes you each on a different path, then you will honor the other's path just as you honor your own. And you will separate for the good of both of you.

You deserve a partner who is truly your friend. Why should you sacrifice your entire life to remain with someone who deadens your senses rather than encouraging all of your senses to come alive? Just because you made a promise at an altar does not mean you have to keep that promise at the cost of your individual growth, self-worth, self-respect, and self-esteem, or your potential, goals, dreams, aspirations, and life purpose.

Marriage can be a wonderful thing; there is nothing intrinsically right or wrong with it. But – and this is a very large but – it is meant to last only as long as the purpose of both partners can be fulfilled. When that purpose – whether it be personal growth, having children, creating something together, learning how to relate – has run its course and the two parties truly become like strangers, it is time to part ways.

Now, this does not mean that when a couple experiences difficult times they should separate. No. Not at all. For to grow to understand, to reach beyond your comfort zone and grow to be your very best both as an individual and as a couple takes work.

Rocky times are a challenge to be acknowledged, worked through, and resolved so you can experience deeper friendship, greater understanding, happier times, and higher levels of life experience together.

Do not think I am saying, "Oh, we disagree, so it's divorce time." No, absolutely not. What I am saying is that if you do not even recognize the person you are married to anymore, if both of you truly have grown and changed in so many areas, on so many levels that you share nothing in common anymore besides a mailing address, that is when the marriage has come to its natural finish. That is when it is time to part ways and to thank the other person for teaching you so much, for helping you grow to be more of who you really are. Throughout a separation and divorce you can display respect and gratitude for all you have learned and shared, and especially for all you have grown.

Honor your feelings. Trust your perceptions. Reach beyond your own desires to understand what the other is trying to communicate. Listen to their words, watch their actions, trust the feelings you pick up from them, and say it all out loud. Do not hold back. Be honest. Your pride is not as important as your personal truth, integrity, and happiness.

For if you place your pride above your personal truth, and you withhold your truth, you will find that you are ultimately alone, without the one you love and even without the love and support of your self. Holding back the real truth leads only to regret.

When you share your truth, even at the expense of your pride, at least you know you did your all. At least you do not live with regret.

Remember always and in all ways: Be true to yourself; be true to the other; dare to say how you feel; dare to express what you think; and dare to live, thrive, and grow, either alone or together. Either way, your desire to be all you can be, can be fulfilled only by honoring your truth and finding the love within to share that truth until you die.

4

SOUL MATES

A Garden of Eden or Growth and Transformation?

Society's current conception of the term "soul mate" is completely contrary to what the term really means.

Imagine two gallons of water taken from the Atlantic Ocean. Both gallons consist of the same energy because they were both part of the same ocean. Yet each gallon will have its own experience separate from the other.

Now imagine a soul in the nonphysical realm that chooses to experience different aspects of itself by inhabiting two different people. Those people consist of the same energy as that one soul: they are soul mates.

Most people on planet Earth do not meet their true soul mates; to do so, to reach the stage where the gift of reunion becomes manifest requires lifetimes of growth and evolution. So far, only about two percent of the human population have actually met their true soul mates.

When most people think of soul mates, they picture a man and woman walking in some eternal garden of mental, emotional, and physical paradise right here on Earth, without a day's worry or tearful eye. But as those who have met their soul mates will attest, this picture of a garden of eternal, blissful paradise is anything but the truth. Yet, once the challenges of their special union have been met successfully, it becomes the truth.

How will you know if yours is indeed a union of soul mates? I will tell you.

HOW IT FEELS TO BE IN A UNION OF SOUL MATES

From the moment you meet, there is a certain familiarity, a knowing you cannot describe in words. In the beginning of your relationship, you do, in fact, feel as if you were in heaven on Earth. You feel love, a union, as if you were a perfect match, which you are. You blend on all levels and in all ways. You feel that you share something unique, something mysterious yet so familiar. You understand each other instinctively, intuitively, and easily, as if you had known each other for eons, as indeed you have.

You see right through to each other's core, and you see each other's best. Each of you is amazed, captivated, even overcome by the other's energy, intelligence, grace, and natural abilities; yet, at the same time, you see all of the other's weaknesses, the areas in which growth is needed. You are not bothered by these weaknesses, however, because you know or believe the other has what it would take to meet these challenges and grow through them.

Your bond is akin to white on rice. You fit together hand in custom-made glove. And, despite being so alike, you embody vast differences. Certainly biological differences: one male, one female. And perhaps intellectual differences: you may be at opposite ends of the intellectual spectrum, with one of you scientifically inclined and the other, spiritual.

Yet in your core you each carry and sustain a comfort level, a feeling of safety and innate understanding you can never put into words. For how can you possibly describe understanding the very depths of one another such a short time after your physical meeting in this life. You cannot. It is inherent. Natural. It simply is.

And it is what you share: your souls, your energy, how in sync you are with each other, how you can sometimes finish each other's sentences, how you have a psychic connection that you have never experienced before. When you are together, you do, in fact, feel you are in your own heaven, your own paradise. You are, after all, with your true other half, so, naturally, you feel as natural with the other and, at times, understand the other more than you understand your self. Do you know why?

Because you chose to meet in this life to grow. This is where the challenges come into play.

HOW THE SOUL-MATE REUNION BRINGS PROFOUND GROWTH AND TRANSFORMATION

A short while after your blissful bond becomes intense, the challenges – the true reasons why you chose to meet again and join physically in this life – come to the surface.

Havoc ensues.

Surely you are not on this Earth to stagnate but to grow. And so ruffles appear within the relationship. But the ruffles have a purpose: they bring to your attention those areas within that each of you must confront, work through, and ultimately heal. No one but your true soul mate could intuitively pull out from your core depths those precise areas that need to grow and heal.

Of course growth is uncomfortable; it is far easier to stagnate. Therefore, you may find yourselves engaged in a tug of war. You may even break up temporarily. But no matter how hard you try, you cannot ever escape the truth of your natural bond. That bond, made up of the energy and chemistry you share with your soul mate, can never be broken.

Because you cannot escape the truth, you have to face it; and when you do, you reap great rewards indeed. When you try to deny or turn away from the reasons you chose to be with your true match, however, you put yourself through unnecessary pain.

It is precisely those areas of growth that you are meant to confront, work through, and heal – the areas your true match has gotten you to notice – that make you to want to run and hide.

But because you can't hide from the truth, you begin, slowly, to realize that yes, you do have issues, core issues that you deserve to heal. And your soul mate sees those issues quite clearly, but they do not bother him or her nearly as much as they bother you. They are simply your deepest challenges; once you meet them, they are healed. Then you experience once again so much of that heaven on Earth the two of you had at the beginning of your relationship.

Denying those challenges is like trying to fight the current of a powerful river. That river is your soul, trying to carry you home to that place of wholeness within where the false views and perceptions of self are finally healed. Fighting this current is fighting the course you chose in order to heal. Meeting your soul mate is the gift that enables you to heal those aspects of your being you have been longing to heal.

This process has been set in motion only because you chose to meet your true other half in this life, to experience the healed, validated, and wonderful being that you are. It is in sharing your growth process with the one who has the same energy you do, the one with whom you fit so perfectly, that you are able to see that process in action. It is then that you experience that heaven-on-earth feeling and, together, experience the perfect fit again. The paradox is that in order to *maintain* that fit, you *must heal* that part within which no longer serves your evolutionary growth.

The patterns of eons past no longer fit. So, in this life, you chose to meet the one who you knew from the beginning was your perfect match.

Fight as you may, that truth shall always be there. And, more than you can imagine, your soul mate is rooting for you to grow. Grow through and heal the false views of self that hinder your evolution, that cause you to stagnate unnecessarily in a life into which you were born to live, experience, explore, thrive, and share the essence of yourself.

You try to run, but you cannot. Your heart longs for that one person, that one true match who understands you so and whose love is so pure. You have known that all along. And though you may feel you do not deserve that love, this feeling is a fallacy.

We all deserve love, soul mate or not.

So, you have challenges that you have chosen to overcome. And there, by your side, is this person who, for some reason you cannot understand, has not told you to go away a long time ago. The reason is that they are a part of you. They share your energy. They are rooting for you. Once you decide to overcome your growth challenges, then and only then will you receive the true bliss of the soul-mate reunion.

The price is honest work on self, removing all old, ingrained, negative patterns that no longer serve you, so you can finally experience the true you, the you that you have been working to achieve for many lifetimes in your evolutionary process. The rewards are indescribable.

Like you, your soul mate has his own issues, which you pull out from within his very core. Every time he tries to run away from facing his responsibility to self, to work through and heal his issues, there you pop up again.

So you are each faced with a choice.

Avoid self growth, and leave your true match behind, never to be forgotten, always to be longed for – or face those aspects within yourself, work on them, and heal them so you are finally and truly free of them. Then you will have your special and perfect match by your side for the remainder of this life.

That is the choice.

To grow or to stagnate?

Now, some couples refuse to grow. They refuse to resolve each of their core issues, which are the true sources of their personal pain. As a result, those soul mates are lost to each other for this life. This is a sad choice for both of them.

And then there are the others, and I do hope you are one of them, who consciously choose to say: No matter how long it takes, I *will* heal within, and I know that as long as I put forth a grain of effort each day, eventually I *will* walk the sands of the most peaceful beach with my true match by my side.

Which do you choose?

It is only your choice.

For if one of the soul mates chooses to grow and the other does not, they must part. Spiritual, universal law forbids that one soul mate may evolve and remain with the other if the other chooses not to evolve. That is the only reason many soul mates do not share the remainder of their lives together.

But they never forget each other. They long for each other, and they yearn and cry for each other in the dark of night when not another soul sees their tears.

The struggle to grow is scary; it is not easy, yet it can and must be done. It will be done. No matter how many lifetimes it takes, eventually you will choose to grow.

After all, what is being asked of you is what you have actually asked the other to come into your life for: To stand by your side and be there for you, so you know that there is one special soul who is there for you always and in all ways; to comfort you when you feel afraid; to be your best friend when the rest of the world turns its back; to challenge you to be your best even as you are loved and accepted when you display your worst.

This is a gift. This is rare. Yet this is what you are entitled to, for you have chosen to grow. You have chosen to heal, and you have done so for important reasons.

Did you ever look within and actually feel afraid of your own individual power? Did you ever truly know, somehow, somewhere, that there is something you came into this life to do, something so beyond the ordinary expressions of individuality of the masses on this planet that you turned away, turned away from your very self?

And when you met your true match, did you see that your soul mate also has an inherent gift for humanity that is unlike most of the masses inhabiting the planet? Did you consider that, like you, your soul mate was at one time afraid of his own power, his own potential – and needed the unconditional acceptance and support of his true match? Did you consider that, to feel secure, he needed to turn to the only one who could understand him and be supportive when the rest of the masses simply could not relate to him?

That is why I say that only about two percent of human beings are actually with their true soul mates in this life now. These are the people who, although not better than the others, have more to contribute to and for the others. They do not have many friends because there is not another except their soul mate to whom they can truly relate.

When you meet your soul mate, you recognize a quality, gifts, potentials, and contributions to humanity and to this universe that the vast majority of others cannot fathom, nor would they care to.

You have chosen to meet to support each other, to be the best friend, the one who understands. You can show every side of yourselves to each other, and it will always be perfectly all right. Soul mates cannot deceive or hide from each other because they can see right through each other.

Your soul mate feels your energy. You communicate on a spiritual level that is difficult to describe; you have an innate, intuitive, psychic connection.

You "know" the other, but your knowing is much more than an understanding; as rational as you try to make it all, you cannot come up with any logical explanation.

On the spiritual, nonphysical side, where your souls exist, your higher selves, you see the colors in your energy patterns change, and this is communicated to you in your physical life. This concept is still too foreign at this point in human evolution for most people to understand. To put it simply, your spiritual selves "see" what you are going through.

In this physical world, when you look at the face of the one you know and love, you can often tell from their expression what they are thinking or how they are feeling. It is the same in the nonphysical side, only it happens with energy patterns of light and color.

So you cannot fool one another. Your growth has to be genuine. As you grow, you feel better about yourself. You also see that your perfect match is right there, has never left your side and never will, as long as you continue to grow, even if only one grain at a time.

THE GRANDER PURPOSE OF THE SOUL MATE REUNION

As the grains of sand accumulate, the higher or grander purposes of the union with your soul mate become more obvious to you both.

You realize – although you may try to look away, afraid of the light on the path you have chosen to take – that those reasons are, in fact, your truest reasons for coming into this life. You realize that you are more than your own personal challenges and growth efforts; you are your essence, and your essence is here on Earth at this precise time and place because it is needed. You are needed, together.

If you look closely, as you would under a microscope, you will see that one half of the soul cannot ever achieve, contribute, or bring forth the results it can when both halves are combined. You are distinct in each of your roles; distinct in each of your vast talents and abilities; yet, you share a common vision. Only when your efforts are combined will you succeed in achieving the purposes you strive to attain.

How can you bake bread without water? How can you bake bread without flour? The flour and water must be combined. Analogously, each soul mate carries the substance that, when combined with the other, produces the results which shall contribute to this universe the very reasons why *you each chose to be born into this life*.

Evolution may appear to be simple, but it is actually quite complex, involving billions of years and billions of energies all working together for the creation of the greater good. Even so, you and your soul mate, combined, are an important part of the evolution of the human species. One soul is no better than another. Every human being is needed to help the species progress.

When you turn away from your own growth, all of humankind pays a great price. As you recognize this, after denial, after trying to run, after all of this nonsense, you say inwardly, "I can't lie to myself anymore, I can't run away anymore, because I know I will regret it all the days of my life."

So you decide to be all you came into this life to be, to be the dearest and best friend to your soul mate; for who other than the one who shares your same energy could better understand your every nuance?

You agree now that you have a purpose. Your first purpose is to grow and heal individually. Only then will your larger purpose be made real. The path shall be very clear. There will be no ambiguity for either of you. You will each know what you are here on this Earth to do. You will each clearly see how perfectly your purposes blend.

You will also come to feel a deep appreciation of how special and rare it is to find a true friend, to have someone in your life whose hand you can always hold no matter what life brings. Their solace shall always bring you solace of your own; their comforting and smiles shall bring you warmth; and their bodies shall always feel as soft and as comfortable as your own skin.

This is the bliss of the soul mate reunion. This is the paradise, the gift, of living in a physical life, creating your own heaven on Earth, as you reach deep within to unleash and finally clear the negativity that previously held you back, the negativity you have surely outgrown.

You will find that neither of you will allow the other to give up, give in, or settle for being less than your very best.

Yes, you can have bad moods. Yes, you may act like two year olds and throw temper tantrums, but as people with responsibility toward yourselves and ultimately toward the advancement of humanity, you will not permit each other to grow complacent or languish in laziness.

So you may find that each of you will always be eager to show the other all you are doing, and this brings joy and excitement into your relationship.

How to find freedom and true inner peace

There is that old saying, "You can run, but you cannot hide."

You may run from your soul mate, you may run from the knowledge of your potential and the inherent gifts you chose to be born into this life to give, but you cannot hide from them. They will always exist within your heart, your mind, and your conscience; and the day will come – perhaps on your last day on this Earth, perhaps this evening – the day will come when you will know who you are, who your soul mate really is, and why you are here. Imagine the joy and exuberance that await you as you come out of hiding, when you stop running, when you look beside you and see your treasure, your gift, the one person who will never let you down. The one person who sees, who knows, who accepts all of you, who shares so much of you. That one person patiently waits for you to allow your best to flow from your being, waits for you to be who you really are.

Nothing more.
Nothing less.
Just pure you.
This is freedom.
This is a gift.

This is your gift to humanity and to this universe: to be you, and to treasure every moment. Release the fear. Be free. Hold nothing back. As you and your soul mate see each other, you recognize how fortunate you are to be able to journey through this life together, for as you know, there are only a few souls to whom you can truly relate. When you have found one another, be glad, and then be all you came here to be. Be yourself, and your soul mate will remain by your side, still doing his own work, in his own way, expressing his own individuality.

The dynamic of the soul mate union works this way:

His issues trigger your growth.
Your growth then challenges him to grow.

Your inner peace must come from your own individual healing, not from the healing of your soul mate. Your peace comes from within. It is from within each of your souls that your deepest truths and life purposes must be revealed, expressed, accepted, understood, and nurtured – first by yourself and then by your soul mate. Once your truths come to the surface, you will find that the love and bond you share will sustain you through the difficult process of individual growth and healing. As you achieve the personal healing of your deepest growth issues, you will feel inner peace. Then, together, you will experience the treasured bliss of the soul-mate union. After all of the turmoil, you will look back and realize that the process was necessary for healing, so you could, in fact, remain together and once again create your own heaven on Earth.

As the sun sets, as the moon glows,
You shall truly know peace
When you see the mirror of you
In the one who shares your soul.

PART II

EMPOWERING SOCIETY AT LARGE

5

EMPOWERING
HUMANITY

Disempowered Children,
Authentically Empowered Adults

What is the process of empowerment? What does the word "power" really mean? Power is not control. And it surely is not money. Many of those who have money certainly do not feel authentic power within. They feel worthless, as if they do not deserve all they have on the outside.

Power is certainly not a title, such as head of state or head of company; these titles are transient, not eternal.

Power is not ownership of anything or anyone, for this, too, fades away with time.

So what is power?

Power is love.

You ask, "Oh, how can this be?" Power is love because to feel power is to have power. To feel love of oneself is *truly* to be *empowered from within*. This is the heart of individual power and the core of transformation.

CHILDHOOD ABUSE AND THE DESTRUCTION OF AUTHENTIC SELF-EMPOWERMENT

The power so many seek is without, outside of their inner being. Some call it the material trap. Yes, this is true. But this false view begins early, perhaps during childhood.

The story I am about to tell is not just my story but the story of so many others. Perhaps it is your story too. It is the story of how disempowerment begins.

When I was very small, until I was about five years old, I felt power. I was so filled with love of life, love of self, curiosity, confidence, and courage. I needed only one thing: love. And I received this love from my mother and natural father. I had belief in self. Like many children, I explored everything that engaged my senses and my attention.

I had the inner power and confidence to display pure self-expression and love of self. It was thrilling to simply be myself.

This was true power. And it was good.

I delighted in the moment; I shared and expressed who I truly was, not in search of approval, not in search of status. At age five I did not even know the concept of status; I didn't have to, because it was not true power, and, so, I did not need it. I was whole, perfect, pure, and complete. I was filled with love of self, as all children are and as they should be.

But something happened to change all that, something that many of you will understand because of your own experience. A new person, my adoptive father, came into my life. And at age six there began a deep and painful change in my perception of self; that new perception persisted into my adult life.

From age six, I was told that I was a nothing, a nobody, dumb, stupid, and dead from the neck up. I began to believe this lie because, as a child, I looked up to adults and respected my adoptive father as an adult.

And, as the years went by, and as his thick, black belt lashed onto my small body, I felt degraded; I felt less than I used to.

No longer did I feel whole, filled with self-love and excitement, and with pure, authentic self-empowerment. Instead, after decades of being told that I was a nothing, I believed I was not good enough.

LOOKING OUTSIDE TO FILL THAT HOLE WITHIN

How could I become "someone" again? Whose approval should I gain?

Perhaps if I was good in school? No, that was not honored or recognized by my peers. In high school, my studies took a back seat. I needed to fit in, to belong, to feel that I was somebody again. So I focused all of my attention on things *outside* of myself.

My looks, boyfriends, listening to the music that the cool kids listened to. Taking the drugs that all the cool kids in high school were taking in the 1970s. Maybe if I was sexier? Would that make me "somebody"? I wondered. Maybe if I was funnier, the class clown? Or the actress, the model, wearing the coolest clothes and hanging out with the coolest people? I knew many rock stars back then. It made me feel I was somebody through association.

My self-esteem was eroded. I felt no self-worth. After so many years of being told I was dumb, stupid, dead from the neck up, a nothing, and a nobody, that became my own view of myself.

It became my personal truth, and so I lived a lie.

Then I thought marriage – being "Mrs. Somebody" – would make me a somebody, but that didn't work either. Owning a large company? I hated it.

Eventually I became an actress. I loved acting; it made me feel again. Acting gave me permission to be and to genuinely express everything I was too afraid to show in the real world.

I joined the Screen Actors Guild and AFTRA. But playing small parts in film, television, and theater still did not fill the void within. I became Oscar driven. I was caught up in my looks. My sense of self-worth was based on whether I got a part. Acting, itself, was one of the most empowering experiences I ever had. It taught me how to genuinely express myself, and how to honestly take in and listen to what I was picking up from others. It taught me to trust my instincts again after so many years of not knowing how to do that.

I met many wonderful people while living in Los Angeles. Becoming active with Women In Film and having dinner with Natalie Cole and Martin Scorcese at the John Huston Awards dinner, which honored Steven Spielberg, I felt for the first time that I did belong. As Natalie and I talked across the table throughout that night, I instinctively felt a kinship with her. I felt I could relate to her before I ever knew her true life story. I thought she was a very special and authentic person. I saw a lot of myself in her during that three-hour dinner. It opened my eyes to the mystery of all the glamour. We were all just people trying to do our best and to bring out our unique gifts.

Once you get past the glamour hype, LA can be an empowering place from the inside out, not the outside in.

SHARING A PATH WITH OTHERS

We usually do feel a kinship with those who travel a similar path. Yet we wonder, how can our personal pain, our false and degrading views of self make a difference? How can our process of healing be a beacon for others to heal as well?

Why, when we are truly good souls, do we have to be the ones to suffer?

Why, when I never once called either of my children a degrading name and never once hit them but gave them only the love and positive attention they deserved – why, then, were they so unjustly ripped away from me?

So many of us on this earth have had only pure hearts yet have been so wrongfully abused. All our tears create a rainbow.

What can we learn from this? What does this have to do with empowering humanity? It has to do with how humanity begins: it begins with the children. Special, whole, and wonderful children. Children with so many beautiful gifts of self to share and express.

Abuse destroys the core of the children. To disempower a child is to disempower humanity. And it is only those abused children who can break the chain when they become adults.

The children who were wronged grow to find resolution within, first for themselves and then for all others. They discover lessons in the fallacies others told them about themselves. They learn that every false message from others breeds more fallacy about self. They find that every truth discovered during healing becomes the gift that sets them free.

"Break the chain: No more child abuse. No more pain."

I created that slogan years ago to break the chain of child abuse. When we honor, respect, encourage, support, and praise all children, then we – and all of humanity – become truly empowered.

MAKING THE DECISION TO HEAL

Those of us who have undergone child abuse, in any form, must heal. We must heal within so that we do not give our pain to the next generation.

As we heal and as we give birth to a new generation of children, we honor them. We honor who they are, complete human beings, just as we all are.

I hope that, in this way, over the next several generations, humanity shall truly be empowered from within. The outside things – money, titles, awards, fans, homes, bank accounts – never fill the void. They never fill that hole within.

Many people in the United States were abused as children. Therefore, many Americans lack self-worth and self-respect, and they seek to fill the emptiness they feel with everything from the outside rather than from within themselves.

As a result, greed has replaced generosity.

If those who have so much felt they would still be worthy if they had a little less, they would be more charitable, and the relationship between the haves and the have-nots would be less strained.

In America, individual power, truth, and justice, have been replaced with honor and respect for the accumulation of wealth, position, and material objects.

Although all people are inherently entitled to have the best of the material world, that is not what true power consists of.

Because of the shift in focus away from what is truly important and of lasting value, injustice grows among the masses. In far too many cases, "justice" can be bought. The needy are looked down upon and considered worthless because they do not possess outward signs of importance.

This false and unnatural shift has disempowered our nation and much of our world.

But truth is eternal; truth shall always win in the end. If you belong to the masses of people who have been wronged, your only choice is to find the truth of your inner being, whole and complete, and, from there, build a new foundation, a new life based on living your joy and your dreams.

It is one thing for me to say this, but you may ask, *How* do I do this? How do I feel whole and complete? My answer is to share with you how I discovered my true individual power, which has been the core of my positive life transformation.

First, I made the decision to honor what I truly wanted to do with my life. Back in 1993 it was to be an actress. I was mocked and ridiculed by relatives, yet despite their telling me to "get a real job," I did what *I* wanted to do, for the first time in my life. I began to feel my worth, being, passion, and core again. At the same time, I was ego driven. I believed if I won an Oscar, I would be validated as a human being. So I had not yet found the core of my individual power, but at least I was on the right path to getting there. Then, during the summer of 1996, just when I *thought* I had it all together, out of the blue I was hit with the custody suit. As I said earlier, I lost everything. My greatest loss was my identity, because it was still focused outward. I was a mother, but I no longer had the joy of raising my children. I was an actress, but I no longer desired to pursue acting because I was emotionally naked, devastated, and numb. I was railroaded by an unjust system, and I felt completely powerless.

During my darkest moments, I decided to become a broadcast journalist so that I could expose injustice within society. My driving force was to expose the injustice surrounding child custody suits, not only for me but for the hundreds of other parents who had called me for help. I felt a true sense of purpose from the inside out, for the first time. I was accepted at the School of Journalism and Mass Communications at Florida International University, and with a 3.8 GPA, I was inducted into Kappa Tau Alpha National Honor Society for Journalism and Mass Communications. I was approved to begin an internship with CNN. Once again, I *thought* that being a CNN journalist made me somebody. I felt secure with this outward status. I didn't know then that the direction of my life was about to change yet again.

Back in 1994, in Los Angeles, a highly spiritual man named Bill Burns told me that I had the ability to disseminate information from God via writing, and that one day I would use this ability to communicate to the masses. At the time, I didn't even understand what Bill meant, and I certainly did not think I had any ability to communicate directly with God. In those days I was only interested in success as a feature film or television actress. A twist of fate brought me both my soul mate and my true life purpose in the summer of 2000. My soul-mate relationship was like the one I described in Chapter 4: a roller coaster of emotional growth that brought me to the heights of joy and the depths of despair as I faced my own weaknesses and growth issues.

I decided to do a writing. I wrote, "Dear God, who *is* this man? Why is he in my life? What are his intentions with me?" And in my writings I received information about which I could have had no possible prior knowledge. I read the writings to my soul mate, and he was shocked at the accuracy. He said, "It is as if you stuck a needle in my brain and extracted fluid. I don't know how you could know all of this." Every day for eighteen months, I did writings. I didn't believe them; I thought I was making it all up. We did an experiment with scientific questions. I asked for scientific information, slept for three days, and received forty-three pages of answers, none of which I could possibly have known. I had never taken a science class. One day in a book store I picked up *A Brief History of Time* by the scientist Stephen Hawking, who, at that time, I had never heard of. (Shows you how knowledgeable I was in the field of science.) When I saw in Hawking's book the same information that had been given to me in my writings, I almost fainted. I was scared to death. After receiving advance information that came to pass in my soul-mate relationship for eighteen months and then receiving the scientific information, I realized I had to believe.

When AOL acquired CNN, hundreds of journalists were laid off, and the internship program was temporarily suspended. I awoke one morning with a pinched nerve in my neck, unable to move. I did a writing and was told it was time to write this book.

As I began to write it, I experienced deep turmoil, confusion, fear, and anxiety about publicly exposing my ability to receive information from God. I was afraid I would be viewed as a new age fruitcake. Having society think of me as a respected journalist with CNN felt much more secure. My turmoil and anxiety was clearly due to fear of what others would think or say. Would I stifle my purpose and take the safer route, or would I be true to myself? What felt true in my heart? Feeling divided within, I had to make a choice. Which would I rather do: bring you your nightly bad news or inspire you? As an author, would I still be able to expose injustice? Would I be able to fear less what others think and honor my own truth?

I chose to follow my heart, and therein lies the core of my life's transformation as well as my individual power.

True individual power does not come from the opinions of others or from being divided within and thus against yourself. It comes from finding the core of your purpose, and that can be found only in your heart.

Others lamented about my so-called failures, iterating that I never won an Oscar or became a broadcast journalist and that now I had a crazy notion of becoming a successful author. At *this* point, I can only smile to myself. Most, if not all, successful people have had to go through the process of finding their truth and sticking to it no matter what others said and no matter how many experiences were deemed as failures. No experience is a failure. You are *not* a failure simply because you have yet to achieve all you desire. Experience is a teacher. You and I have simply learned from our experiences. The fateful twists of life amid our tragedies are what bring us our greatest strength and wisdom. You cannot *ever* judge your *self* as a failure simply because you have not yet succeeded. Perhaps you are preparing for your success by way of varied life experiences.

To succeed, see the ideal life you long for as complete. Know that because you deserve all of your joys to be made manifest, they shall be.

With resolve, understanding, and decisiveness, you can create the life you want and deserve, and you will stop buying into the belief that you are "less than" any other, no matter how much he or she may possess.

Compare yourself to no other, but gain inspiration from the few who have shared their pain and have overcome their darkest hour to shine again as the children they once were.

The only difference between them and you is an inner resolve, a decision backed with sheer will, vision, determination, and consistency. That is the only difference. In finding and honoring my truest self, I feel younger than I ever have. I feel like the child I once was.

We are all children. We are all part of humanity, and we are all whole and complete within.

If you think you are a nothing, then you yearn for something –
anything – to change that view of yourself, to release yourself
from this lie so you may live your truth again.

Your truth consists of all the qualities, talents, abilities, and at-
tributes you were born with; they express your essence, and they
are to be used to your liking and your joy. Then you will be able to
erase the bleak picture you may have had of your life. Your essence is your authentic self-empowerment. This is love: love of
self, from the inside out.

Find a picture of yourself from a time when you felt you were
pure within, when you felt that purity and wholeness. That is still
who you are. You have not changed. You have learned, and you
have grown. But so much of that learning has been false. You
learned lies. And so did I. We have to undo the lies. We have to re-
learn the truth from the inside out. What follows is a process I
learned to find my love of self again at a time when I hated myself
the most.

MIRROR, MIRROR ON THE WALL

Many years ago in Los Angeles, that same wonderful man named
Bill Burns taught me a technique that made a difference in my
life. I was to name at least three good qualities about myself every
day and actually do a dialogue with myself in the mirror.

Now, when he suggested this to me, the last place I wanted to
look was in a mirror. Not because I didn't like my face – I knew I
had a pretty face – but because I had learned falsehoods that
made me abhor my inner self.

When I looked at myself in the mirror, what I really wanted to
say was, "F___ you, you dumb piece of shit. You're a nothing,
you're stupid, and I hate you, bitch."

That was what I believed about myself until 1994.

Bill suggested that I find qualities stemming from my actions,
qualities that I could feel proud of, at least three times a day. It did
not matter what the qualities were as long as they were positive.

So on the first day, I observed my actions and found three positive qualities in them. Going to work was responsible. Hugging my children was loving. Taking a shower was being clean. Then I had to look in the mirror at this person I despised and tell myself I was responsible, loving, and clean.

Bill knew that if I told myself airy-fairy affirmations, such as "I love me," the process wouldn't work because I would not believe those statements. I hated me. But when I looked at myself in the mirror and told myself the truth based upon my actual, observable actions, I could believe it.

I was to repeat this process two or three times each day.

In the beginning, the scene would go something like this: I would go up to the mirror, see my face, say: "F___ you, bitch. OK, you are responsible, loving, and clean. Bye."

But Bill explained that as the days went by, I was becoming a *friend* to *me* again. I was getting through the false views; in fact, I was not a bitch; I was a loving person, a genuine person. But it took a lot of conscious effort to chip away the lies I believed about myself and to finally start to like myself again, just as I did when I was five years old. Before the child abuse began.

Now, today, the lies are gone. There are memories, but I no longer hate myself. I also do not think I am any better than anyone else. Now, today, I simply feel more love and appreciation for the goodness that I am; and I learned to stop insulting myself and cutting myself down.

If someone else were to call you those degrading names you call yourself, there would surely be a nasty scene.

Bill told me to never again view myself in a degrading way and to stop insulting myself. Oh, yes, I make mistakes just about every day of my life. And that is OK, for to expect yourself to be perfect is to abuse yourself.

We learn from imperfection, not perfection. We grow from adversity, not from ease. But we deserve ease.

So the key to empowering yourself is to look for the *seed of opportunity* in every seeming tragedy, every happening that is unpleasant or not to your liking. The seed is always there.

Tragedy – loss of a certain belief, identity, self-perception, loss of a person, a career, a home – leads to genuine life renewal.

Life cannot renew itself when what must yield refuses to give way. The chaos of tragedy and loss often precedes growth. The fabric of our entire reality may crumble before our eyes, bringing us to the depths of despair.

Yet there will be a new dawn.

TRAGEDY AND SOCIAL CHANGE

The tragedy of so many mothers losing their precious children in automobile accidents that resulted from drinking and driving led to the establishment of MADD and changes in the law; millions of lives have since been saved.

Before seat belts and air bags became mandatory, many people were needlessly maimed or killed in car accidents. These tragedies led to changes that have saved others from the same fate.

Since my deeply unjust loss of primary custody of my children, I have had years of communication with other single parents, predominately mothers, who, after divorce, unjustly lost custody of their children also. In an overwhelming majority of cases, the mothers lacked the exorbitant amounts of money required for continuous legal representation during lengthy custody litigation suits. This problem now affects more and more women nationwide.

I hope to raise public debate over this travesty. Current post-dissolution custody laws must be amended at the federal level because many parents move from one state to another, thereby voiding many court decisions as jurisdiction changes.

Federally, there must be documented proof that a parent has caused abuse, neglect, harm, or danger to his or her child to warrant a permanent change in residential or primary custody.

Without such proof, the need for custody litigation would be eliminated.

Children are the greatest victims in bitter custody battles. New federal law should be established requiring that, when primary custody changes, the primary custodial parent provide the children with weekly emotional counseling for at least three months, to help the children heal the scars of their unjust pain.

This will do much to help prevent violence in our society. Without therapeutic counseling, many of these children grow into adults whose lives are either a living hell within or destructive on the outside, and that destruction is perpetrated on others.

More such issues are discussed in the next chapter.

THE ROOT OF AUTHENTIC EMPOWERMENT

Growth, life renewal, change, and honoring our ability to do so create authentic self-empowerment. If we lived in a perfect world, we would each be sitting on our own rainbow, eating ice cream all day.

But we *do* have the individual power to create rainbows from the rivers of tears we have shed.

I understand that amending child custody laws may not be a cause that touches your heart, nor does it have to. This is my voice, which I now honor, and I choose to create changes to resolve a problem that has fallen on deaf ears for far too long.

You have a voice too.

If something in your life has created pain, please realize that you have an opportunity to *do* something about it.

You don't have to act today. We are not usually effective in the midst of turmoil. I did not have the inner strength to move forward in an authentically empowered way until a full year after my custody case was final.

I did not have it all laid out. Some people live one step at a time. Others need a long-term plan. Often, the plan changes.

Welcome the changes. If they are unpleasant, grieve, feel, and trust that there *is* a new dawn once we *decide* to face the light of the path before us.

So, we must empower humanity by empowering ourselves.

We must love our children by loving and sharing ourselves.

We must help ourselves heal, if only by saying kind remarks to ourselves in the mirror.

We must honor and respect our children by first honoring and respecting our own ability, our capacity to make a difference for ourselves.

Our children can feel love of self and grow to extend that love to others only when we show them *how* by our example.

To create a nation and a world where humanity is empowered, loved, respected, and cared for, each of our examples is crucial.

Do not judge yourself or others based on material wealth but on who you are. Because you are a human being, you are worthy of dignity and worthy of respect.

Authentic empowerment of humanity can come only from within.

Our contributions to uplift our own lives must flow from our hearts. Only then will we truly and naturally reach beyond the focus on self to share our contributions with others. When we dare to claim empowerment as our birthright, we help others – even those we may not know but whose lives we have somehow touched – to empower themselves as well. You have within your life experience the seeds for profound transformation. Your resolve to live according to the expectations and validation of others will be followed by your children. Your inner resolve to live authentically will also be followed by your children. When you stop abusing yourself, stop judging and putting yourself down, you will teach your children that it is OK to make mistakes. It is OK to change direction. It is OK to simply be who you are, and that is truly good enough.

6

POLITICAL
RESPONSIBILITY

*Getting to the Heart of Critical
Issues*

*I pledge allegiance to the flag of the United Nations of the
World, and to the people for which it stands, one world,
under God, indivisible, with liberty and justice for all.*

Does it really matter where on this earth a father or mother holds
or mourns for his or her child? Aren't all emotions international,
the same for all humankind? Do they not cross a certain river or
mountain or border? When one parent buries a child killed by
war, doesn't every parent on planet Earth feel the pain and cry
tears of understanding and compassion?

When nations were smaller, eons ago, they shared a common
bond: survival. Then conquerors became heroes, brutalizing,
murdering, raping, burning, and stealing the land and the lives of
those who lived on the property they sought to gain, only to see it
fall out of their control again, eventually.

Political power and monetary wealth have now become the
conquerors. Power plays a major role in politics. And it is those
with money who wield power. To whom do they pledge allegiance? To which people under God?

The word "political" certainly carries a connotation of partisanship; and to combine the word "political" with the word "responsibility" almost conveys an oxymoron.

The small group of people who think they hold power over the sea of humanity within their borders devour the large group as if they were shrimp. Sadly, far too many politicians do not see or understand on a deeply personal level the suffering of the masses, not even the masses within their own legislative districts.

Far too many cries fall on deaf ears. Far too many people who may have unintentionally wronged others because of the fine print on a contract – people who had no malice in their hearts but could not afford legal representation on a grand scale – are convicted as if they intended to commit grand larceny. I am neither for nor against politics. I simply observe that many changes need to take place to assure that there be "liberty and justice for all."

The United States of America is a wonderful model of individual freedom and democracy that can, with diplomacy and sincere open dialogue, spread worldwide.

How? By adding other willing nations to the union and calling them "nation states" within the jurisdiction of the United States of America. Why? Take a look at Somalia and other small nations whose populations are dying of starvation. Allowing those poorest countries to become part of the U.S. would have an empowering impact on a global scale and should be seen not as a strategic move toward military might but as a move toward humanitarian integrity.

If we open our hearts, the goodness will return to us. Not only would we be helping those poorest nations most in need but we would be setting an example for other wealthy democracies that could follow our lead.

A WORLD WITHOUT BORDERS

In this age of the World Wide Web and satellites that provide instantaneous global communication, does it not seem ludicrous to have borders? News networks like CNN have bureaus worldwide. Many large, wealthy companies have facilities worldwide. A number of them maintain factories in the poorest nations and exploit starving people to save money. Is this fair? You know in your heart it is not.

There are international colleges and year-abroad programs that obtain astounding results in teaching young people to communicate with students from different lands to appreciate their differences and similarities.

My freshman year was spent at Franklin College, an American school in Lugano, Switzerland, that offers programs in international studies. Yes, I experienced culture shock in 1981 when I visited places such as Russia. But I also learned about vastly different systems of life and survival. I realized then how humanity must embrace all others rather than uphold separation.

My friends were students from Iraq, Iran, Saudi Arabia, Turkey, India, Greece, Malta, Japan, Sweden, Switzerland, Italy, France, and several other countries. We were the elite of the world. We came from wealthy families, some of whom had great political power. But for a Jewish-Italian-American from Queens, New York, to remain best friends with students from Iraq, Iran, and Saudi Arabia for more than twenty years – does that not tell you we really can be a world without borders?

We are all members of humankind. As eighteen- and nineteen-year-old students, we were just a group of wealthy jet-setters who were learning, traveling the world, sharing friendship, and having a ball. Our friendships were genuine regardless of the nations we represented. There were no stereotypes, no prejudices or politics.

Many of my friends' parents were heads of their nations, some attended OPEC meetings, but the parents all got along because they shared a common connection: surviving their children's teen-age years.

If national borders were eliminated, a good percentage of the money that is budgeted for the military could be used to help *uplift* humanity. Instead of using money to protect borders, to maintain separation and breed even more intolerance, governments could use it to feed the hungry and to build more schools and homes and hospitals.

The countries of Europe are similar in size to the states in the U.S. Traveling from Switzerland to Italy is similar to traveling from Georgia to Florida. The European nations could be combined into a single nation state that was part of the United Nations of Earth. The U.S. could also be a nation state belonging to the United Nations of Earth, as could the Middle East.

As for Jerusalem, it could be a neutral zone, as neutral as Lugano, Switzerland, with people of all faiths keeping their historical sites. No one political party or group of people can claim ownership over this region. To kill children in battles for the land is obscene. People cannot take the land with them when they die – a fact often overlooked during the process of killing for it. This is a precious, sacred land that belongs to all who wish to claim it. People of all faiths and all ethnicities are entitled to care for it, preserve it, and enjoy it for as long as they live.

Instead of trying to attain security for a few, why not build bridges between all people?

Although many countries may not yet be ready to embrace this concept of acceptance, we can nonetheless begin to put it into action right here at home in the U.S.

It seems to me that most political parties and governments act in the interests of only a small part of their constituents: those who have "Inc." after their names. As mergers multiply, corporations become larger and larger, and their leaders appear to exert much power over the government.

TO KILL OR NOT TO KILL

There are people in the United States on death row, people convicted of murder and sentenced to die. Yet, *many of them are innocent.* Many of them have been railroaded within the system that is supposed to mete out justice. Yes, they were found guilty in courts of law. But why, after DNA testing was done, have so many of them been released? Other innocent people remain on death row, and this in itself is a crime.

The world's major religions agree with the commandment "Thou shall not kill." Who, then, gives a judge or a jury the right to condemn a person to death? Who gives the state the right to execute that condemned person? Certainly not God.

When you give people a one-way ticket out of this life via injection, electrocution, hanging, or any other means, you do not make them pay for their crime. No. Instead, you allow them to escape from paying.

Death row should be eliminated. Let those now on death row serve life terms, and let DNA testing determine where innocence lies, whenever possible. Free those who are innocent, and compensate them for the time they have been unjustly imprisoned. To free an innocent person without adequate financial compensation that will allow him to resume normal life with some measure of dignity is in itself a shameful crime committed by the government that imposed the death sentence wrongly.

I strongly believe that the commandment "Thou shall not kill" means we must not kill persons already born. I do not believe it refers to fetuses in the first trimester. Abortion is *not* a crime. *A woman is entitled to choice.*

No woman is ever happy before, during, or after an abortion. In all cases, abortions are done out of necessity. Children, teenagers, should not be forced to become parents regardless of how they became pregnant. Rape victims should not be forced to bear the fruit of violence. No unwanted child should be brought into this world. Before you act as judge and jury, try walking in the shoes of the woman or young girl whose life is in torment and turmoil. Then, if you, personally, cannot be a parent to the unborn fetus, stop proclaiming that fetus's right to life while you seek to *destroy* the life of the woman or young girl who is already here.

Of course I strongly advocate birth control and the RU486 morning-after pill, both of which can certainly help prevent the need for abortion.

A person's right to life, liberty, and the pursuit of happiness must not be ended because you view what they do, how they live, or to whom they pray as "wrong." Every person on Earth does not have to agree with your views or beliefs.

On September 11, 2001, the terrorists sincerely believed they were justified in their acts of blowing up buildings and people. They believed they were serving God. Likewise, here in the U.S., those Christians who vehemently proclaim the right to life have blown up abortion clinics and killed innocent people. They too sincerely believed they were serving God. Unfortunately, history provides a litany of examples in which one group killed another in the name of religion, from the Crusades to the Holocaust to the events in the Middle East and Ireland today. But no religious leader, from Jesus to Buddha to Mohammed, condoned killing in his name. People who kill supposedly in the name of God actually serve their own need: the need to control the beliefs of others.

No one has the right to kill any human being except in self-defense.

POLITICS IN THE UNITED STATES

The mayhem involved in the U.S. presidential election in 2000 produced significant uncertainty among the American people with respect to their constitutional right to elect representatives to government. Many people were left hanging, along with the scores of "hanging chads."

The nation became the butt of jokes worldwide, jokes that clearly resulted from the surreptitious, archaic, and failing methods by which our elections are held. Our government failed us.

Perhaps if our political parties had spent less money on banquets, lobster dinners, limousines, and victory celebrations and more on lobbying for efficient electronic voting equipment, we would have more cause to celebrate.

Our voting system is not the only thing that needs to be over-hauled. We need to pay more attention to whether our politicians' values truly come from their hearts. Status and power seem to have taken precedence over fairness, honesty, and integrity among many who seek to represent the people of the United States.

The priorities of many United States politicians need to be carefully scrutinized. For example, given the importance of the national budget and the various good causes that do not receive enough funding, was it necessary to spend so many of our tax-payer dollars on an investigation into the private life of a president? Bill Clinton is a wonderful statesman. As president, he sought to help uplift the poor and oppressed. He continues to seek ways to genuinely help empower *the people*. Did the Clinton-Lewinsky investigation truly serve the people?

How can the government – those who supposedly represent the wishes and needs of the people – cut spending on computers for our school children and instead fund legal action and the publication of reports about an investigation that does not serve any constructive purpose for the people it claims to represent?

This is not government; this is politics, and dirty politics at that. To spend millions of tax dollars looking into a president's personal life is a crime against the taxpayers. Think of all the homeless people, hungry children, and others who could have been helped with that money.

Whose interests do the politicians truly serve? It seems that they are self-serving, which is why their power cannot last. Spiri-tual politicians are those who serve from their hearts, with the in-tent of bringing justice to all people. They do not gain money and power by taking it from the needy. They do not commit injustice in the name of justice. Instead of creating their own noise, they listen to the cries of the people they represent who feel powerless.

Spiritual politicians work tirelessly to help the people. I wish there were more of them. The effect of their hard work will be felt for generations. Their goodness shall always be remembered; their deeds are not for naught. They are an example of individual power. They use their hearts as a catalyst for justice. In so doing, they uplift and transform the lives of those within their legislative districts.

But there are others, politicians who are blinded by greed, status, position, authority, money, clout, and influence. They have closed their hearts, covered their eyes, and hardened their conscience. They have become everything other than who they came on to this earth to be: their real selves.

There is a way, however, by which they can redeem themselves. It is called bi-partisanship. If all the politicians worked together for the common good of the people instead of for their own gain, imagine how much could be accomplished. For example, a health care system could be put in place so that not one citizen would ever again go without medical care. All tax money now spent on unnecessary frills could be used for education and scholarships. The vast financial resources of the government, if properly and humanely directed, could work to help politicians fulfill their main responsibility: improving life for the human beings they represent.

ORDER IN THE COURT

The nightmare of injustice I experienced in regard to custody of my children was not unique. It happens to parents in family courts all over the United States. I can only tell you about my own experience.

In Broward County, Florida, the family court judge in charge of my custody case appointed a guardian ad litem (which means guardian at law). I'll call her Ms. Jonas.

Guardians ad litem are frequently appointed in custody cases. Their purpose is to look out for the best interests of the children during legal proceedings. They act as advocates for the children. They may investigate the situation and make recommendations to the court. Most commonly, the guardians are volunteers who are not paid for their services. The judge in my case, a fine woman, appointed Ms. Jonas as the guardian. Ms. Jonas was a private attorney whose fee to oversee my custody case was $150 per hour. The judge ordered that the fee was to be split evenly between my former husband and me. The judge had full faith in Ms. Jonas. She accepted her recommendations as absolute truth, without question. As a result, in essence, Ms. Jonas became the judge. Furthermore, there was not an impartial third party to whom I could report wrongdoings by Ms. Jonas. Is that justice?

Of course I could not afford to pay half of Ms. Jonas's fee. I didn't even have enough money for food. I had come from California to Florida on a visit; my whole life was in a storage bin. In examining her invoices, I noticed that the notations contained pure lies and half truths. Everything was slanted in favor of my former husband, who, at the time, had plenty of money and was able to pay her invoices with ease, on time, every month.

On Mother's Day in 1997 my ex-husband would not let me see my children. Thinking this was not right, I phoned Ms. Jonas. Her exact words to me were: "Maybe if you paid me some of the money you owed me, I would lean a little more in your direction." Of course my mouth dropped open. This was blackmail. I was horrified. I replied, "What?" And she said, "Do you understand me?" As shocked and scared as I was, I said, "Yes."

The problems continued. For example, she brought her son over to my ex-husband's house one Sunday to spend the afternoon swimming in his backyard pool with my two children – and charged me for my share of this "visit." I was very angry.

Furthermore, Ms. Jonas's final report to the court contained lies, half-truths, and omissions of the truth all of which favored her financial source, my ex-husband. She lied about my bringing the children to school late. The school records, which I obtained, showed no tardies at all.

The truth, which I filed in a complaint against Ms. Jonas with the Florida Bar, was all swept under the rug.

Why do I write about this here? Because it speaks to the kind of injustice that is perpetrated throughout our legal system.

Guardians ad litem should not be paid by the parties involved so that they can not be influenced by money. Furthermore, there should be someone within the family court system to whom a report of wrongdoing can be given concerning any improper conduct by the guardian ad litem.

In my case, the judge never knew what was going on behind her back. She simply accepted Ms. Jonas's statements as true. Many judges are not aware of the extent of injustice in their courts. As a result, many innocent people are railroaded within the very system that should be protecting them. The courts seem to favor those who carry only one coin, not that of truth but of the almighty dollar.

As a result of this travesty, I sent a gender neutral, bipartisan bill to Congress entitled "The Family Justice Post-Dissolution Primary Caregiver Act." Its purpose is to determine if a custody battle after divorce is warranted; to protect children from being removed from safe, loving single parents unjustly; and to prevent unnecessary custody battles through careful pretesting and evaluation of all parties. If the children are found to be in no danger, then the need for a custody battle is pointless. Good single parents who cannot afford exorbitant legal fees will no longer be railroaded. If the children *are* found to be in danger, then the custody suit would of course continue as it should.

But the greatest injustice of all was committed not against me but against my son, who should have been protected by the guardian ad litem who supposedly was appointed to look after his best interests.

My son was only nine months old when his father and I got divorced. I raised him until he was six years old, when he was suddenly ripped away from me. I could see, as any mother could, the pain in his eyes. I knew he needed counseling to help him adjust. I pleaded with Ms. Jonas to have counseling provided for my son. His father was certainly wealthy enough to pay for it. But because my former husband "did not believe in counseling," Ms. Jonas refused my request. Letters I sent to the judge about this were thrown into my file unread.

My son never received the counseling he needed to heal the deep scars he bears within. This was my greatest pain: to see my child hurt, to plead for help for him, and to be refused, all supposedly in the name of his best interests. This was a crime within the judicial system.

I discovered my individual power in the heart of my greatest pain. In so doing, I sent another bill to Congress entitled "American People for Family Justice Child Custody Counseling Act." Its purpose is to rally bipartisan support to ensure that any child who is removed from the custody of one parent or primary caregiver and placed into the physical custody of another parent or primary caregiver, no matter what the circumstances, receive three to six months of private emotional counseling to be paid for by the primary custodial caregiver to heal the child's pain.

I strongly believe *this* is justice for the children.

Another child I know was also a victim of the judicial system. Her mother was a crack addict. The state awarded custody of the five-year-old girl to the maternal grandparents and imposed a "no contact" order, forbidding the grandmother any contact with the mother of the child. When the mother telephoned the house, naturally the grandmother picked up the phone. In so doing, she unintentionally disobeyed the court's order. The grandmother had a conversation with her daughter, who was in a drug rehabilitation treatment program. Then a guardian of the court asked the child if she had had any contact with her mother. She said, "No, but my grandma spoke to her on the phone." The guardian told that to the judge, who immediately removed the child from the safe, loving care of her maternal grandparents and placed her with a foster family. In foster care, the child was repeatedly sexually molested.

In response to that injustice, I have sent a bill to Congress entitled "The Child Protection from Foster Care Act." Its purpose is to protect children from being removed from the loving care of family members when their natural parents do not have custody and when no actual harm is being perpetrated on the children. The foster care system must be amended such that, unless actual harm is being committed against them, children would not be taken away from loving relatives and placed in foster care.

To whom should the justice system be responsible? Not to the politicians, even though judges may be appointed by them. No. Like the politicians themselves, members of the justice system must be responsible to the people.

We cannot any longer ignore the cries, pleas, tears, and traumas of the masses who are born with an inherent right to life, liberty, and the pursuit of happiness. We cannot continue to serve our own interests or the interests of partisan politics at the expense of liberty and justice for all.

If you are working in any capacity within the judicial system, you may know in your heart where you have wronged or gone astray, where you have erred. If you can face it, own up to it, acknowledge it, even if only to yourself, you can decide at this very moment to create a new start from within you. Your decision to change can make a profound and positive difference.

You do not have to go backwards. If there is something you can do to right a wrong, then by all means do so.

But if you can only begin from where you are at this very moment, then that shall suffice.

Begin anew. Renew your mind, open your heart, do not judge others. Let your conscience and not your bank account be your guide.

If you don't make those changes, in the end you will feel you are rotting away from the inside out. This is the material trap. The inside loses its heart, soul, purity, and compassion, and rots with greed.

The transformative power of your actions can cause your entire life to change course. You can also save a child's life from being destroyed. If we each found the heart of our authentic individual power and used it for the uplifting of our own selves and the greater good of all, we could cause an entire nation to flourish with democracy, an entire world to be free to enjoy humanity's birthright of life, liberty, and the pursuit of happiness. Your goodness, the goodness you were born with, can have a profound and immeasurable positive impact on the world. You simply have to use it. If only you would seek within, there, in your heart, you would find the answer, the key to open a whole new world. Humanity has yet to see this new world, but see it she shall. For humanity is goodness, if only we decide to believe in it and act on the goodness within ourselves.

From sea to shining sea,
Liberty and justice for all is political responsibility.

7

TRANSFORMING YOUR PAIN TO POSITIVE POWER

*M*any if not most nonprofit foundations begin when one or a few people decide to make a difference as a result of their pain. They became empowered rather than destroyed. As a result, they grow to become beacons for others whose pain they can genuinely understand.

A foundation holds the fabric, the structure, the hope, and the promise of life. A foundation for the common good receives from the people, for the people.

What need is a foundation created to fulfill? What promise does it hold for others?

To build a nonprofit foundation is perhaps one of the greatest contributions from humanity for humanity. Many foundations have grown out of the tears, the broken hopes, and the tragedies of those who built them from scratch. To use pain and disaster, out of the compassion in one's own heart, to bring forth good for others so they shall never know of their pain again – that is the goodness of humanity.

And, yes, humanity is basically good, especially during adversity. Adversity presents the need to overcome, to find a way to replace the trouble with a cure, a hope, a promise.

Is there an area in life where you have undergone hardship, a hardship felt by many others? You can begin a new, nonprofit foundation by requesting a grant from a large for-profit company; and through that new foundation, you can begin to sow the seeds of good to replace the havoc of disaster.

Understandably, people usually do not donate money to foundations unless the causes represented have touched their lives. Most people want to prevent pain from happening to others, yet they do not follow through. Once you find the vision and the perseverance to turn your idea into a physical reality, once you get the ball rolling, it can, indeed, roll right into the lap of many who truly need what you offer.

In my own life, I have felt the pain many single parents face when trying to raise children with few resources. I understand how overwhelming responsible positive parenting can be when we have so much to do and few, if any, people to turn to for support or guidance.

For this reason, I am starting the Rose Foundation. The foundation will distribute educational materials to parents who are at risk of becoming homeless – materials I will co-write with other experts in the fields of psychology, life skills, and positive parenting. Seminars that I present, along with a positive-parenting method I created, called Star Kids, will help educate single parents on how to fulfill their dreams and raise children with positive reinforcement rather than negative punishment.

The goal of the Rose foundation is to educate parents – to teach them how to change their lives from a negative spiral of depression and dysfunction to a thriving example from which their children can learn.

To that end, the Rose Foundation will provide scholarships to parents who want to better their lives and the lives of their children. Children whose lives have been torn apart by family dissolution will receive funds for summer camp and for emotional counseling to help them heal their pain.

Ending the downward spiral that leads to homelessness can be accomplished only through education. The welfare of each person will come from self-sufficiency rather than from dependence on limited outside sources. Each adult will learn how to thrive. As a result, each child will thrive and create a role model for the next generation to follow.

How you can use this idea

Perhaps you own a restaurant. You could set up a nonprofit foundation, receive grant money, and use it to donate food to homeless shelters or to neighborhood people who are ill or out of work. You do not have to give away everything you own or deplete your holdings. Rather, you can find ways to use what you have to help others.

Turning a volunteer organization into a nonprofit foundation

People who operate foundations must take a salary. Your employees must be paid for their work. So I am not speaking of a volunteer organization. Of course volunteer services are welcome and wonderful. But there is an unnatural tilt of the scales in our American society from corporations with soaring corporate profits to volunteer organizations where the cause and the voice behind the cause are muted by the need of the people simply to eat. You cannot expect people to give tirelessly of their time, energy, talents, or money when doing so causes a strain on their lives.

Rather than request so many to volunteer, create a foundation and pay people for the services they give to it.

If there is a cause that touches your heart and captivates your mind, know that you are not alone in this universe. That cause will also touch many others.

When thinking of a foundation, try to be as practical and specific as possible about what you seek to offer so donors can see exactly how their money will help.

Find experts in management, public relations, fund-raising, and marketing. Choose qualified people to serve on your board of directors and on an advisory board, which will guide you but will not be involved in the day-to-day running of your organization.

Bring many people to the table so you are not alone. You will find that if your motive is pure, to genuinely be of help and service, you will naturally attract the people into your life who can answer your questions, fill the jobs offered by your foundation, and help you to build it.

There is a saying that goes, "Someone is looking for exactly what you have." You will always meet the right people, whether in person, online, through friends, or in a chance encounter at a bookstore. You will be guided to precisely where you need to be in order to receive the help or information you require to move along, one step at a time.

What has happened in your life that you can turn into a positive experience for others? Might you create a new kind of museum, a school, a program? Might you simply set up a contact list of people in your field that a person just starting out can access online? Might you offer helpful information on your own Web page?

Take your joys, your struggles, your lessons, your hardships, pains, triumphs, or tragedies and create something good out of them to help others.

THE COMPETITION FALLACY

So many people falsely think that if they help another, they are helping the competition. This scarcity perspective breeds greed and insecurity; ultimately, people who hold it will realize that had they not been helped at certain times, they would not have had the opportunity to be where they are today.

Now, if where you are today is the last place you would like to be, then this moment is your starting point, the important place from which you will create a way to shine again – to achieve, produce, and share the lessons you have learned as a result of your hardship.

Perhaps you feel happy about where you are today, perhaps you have come that far. Then this too is your time to create a way to help others. Share *how* you achieved your success. You will not be "giving your secrets away"; instead you will find that you are helping so many people uplift themselves that the rewards and recognition you receive will be immeasurable.

A special woman named Arielle Ford is a well-known, highly respected publicist. Because I did not yet have a publishing contract while writing this book, she could not take me on as a client. But I knew I needed publicity to ensure that the messages in this book would reach you. Arielle offers a taped seminar series called "Book Publicity University." It is phenomenal. She created it for authors who cannot afford to hire a publicist. Ironically, on one of the tapes she describes a recurring dream in which she shares her publicity secrets and know-how with others. At the time those dreams occurred, she thought, "What a nightmare." When I listened to this, I smiled. Her "nightmare" was the answer to my prayers. Thank you, Arielle!

If you take a lit candle and walk into a room with one hundred people, each holding an unlit candle, and you touch your flame to the wick of another candle, you create more light. You do not lose anything by giving unto another. And as all the people in the room realize this, their light touches another until all one hundred candles are lit. The room is filled with light. Yet you always and forever will retain your own.

That is the process and the power of giving. You do have so much more when you give and so do so many others. If you held onto your single lit candle and were afraid to lose your light by giving to another, your fear would prevent you from seeing the difference you can make. Your fear stems from your belief that you will lose what you have if you give to another.

Please realize you are not meant to give all you have away, but you can certainly contribute: simple advice, a phone call, an answer to a letter. When you cooperate, you give. When you lend an ear, you give friendship or comfort. Time is a valuable gift. Do not deplete your life, however, if you are not being given to in return.

A TIME TO GIVE AND A TIME TO RECEIVE

Many foundations burn out their volunteers by asking them to give and give tirelessly when they are not being given to in return.

Food cannot be bought with the feelings of joy and happiness produced by acting selflessly.

Certainly you may give of your time as much as you can afford to give; however, if you need money to live, you cannot expect yourself to give all of your time while your basic needs go unmet. So, at certain times in life we can give more than at other times. Sometimes we can give of our time. Sometimes we can give of our money. Sometimes we cannot give at all, and at those times we may need to receive.

Many people who give do not feel comfortable receiving, yet this is the harvest of life. You plant – give – into the earth, and then you reap a harvest.

When I was a married, stay-at-home mom, I donated to a charity in my community. I cooked dinner for needy families. I gave from my heart, and it felt good. When I lost custody of my children, I completely fell apart. I was evicted from my apartment, and I did not have money to buy food. I found myself at the door of the same charity I had donated to years earlier. They helped me. They gave me money for food. I felt completely humiliated, and yet, I learned a lesson: it is okay to receive. Receiving does not make me a less worthy person. I had to stop looking down on myself because I needed to receive. I also realized in hindsight that it gave another human being the opportunity to give to me. Giving and receiving are both blessings for each person. Neither is above the other.

Life ebbs and flows. So if the circumstances in your life are such that you cannot give freely right now, this is okay. You must take care of your own needs.

Perhaps you can still give but be paid in return. Perhaps your gift is a smile or an understanding ear. Those too are gifts. For there must be an equal give-and-take in life; it is time people stopped placing more value on the almighty dollar than on the way they relate to others.

I know many people who have a great deal of money. Many of them do not give; they hold on to their money for dear life. When they learn that all of their money cannot buy their health or a loved one, perhaps then they will stop valuing money more than people.

THE ANSWER TO HUMANKIND'S GREATEST QUESTION

As disaster strikes, as havoc ensues, the turmoil brings forth inward searching, a searching with the greatest question asked by humankind: Why? Why do bad things happen to good people?

Why does tragedy befall those who are good? Why does misfortune prey on those who do not seek to find a harsh reality but are subject to the pain many view as being wrongfully placed – on the good, rather than the evil?

The answer to this eternal question contains eternal truth.

The answer is: because those who are good will find a solution, a remedy, so that the tragedy will never strike others or themselves again.

They are the ones who have a heart, who have compassion, who seek to bring justice and ease into lives in which injustice and tragic hardship previously prevailed. Tragedy falls on the special few so that there can be a solution for the many.

You know in your heart the pains you have undergone, and you also know all of the good you are bringing or can bring into the lives of others as a result.

So this is the answer. Why you? Because you chose this as your reality, your sacrifice, with full agreement of the souls of those who have also undergone tragedies that had such a vast impact on your life. They agreed to do this. Their worthy lives acted as catalysts for powerful and positive growth and change, for the highest betterment of all. Many who have passed over to the spiritual or nonphysical side are in a better place, for they chose to uplift humanity prior to their incarnation into this life. And you made a soul agreement with them to carry the torch of their light, their love, their tremendous sacrifice, so no other shall have to undergo the pains they endured to ensure that lasting change would take place among the masses. That is why I say: Look for the gift in the tragedy. The seed is there. The seed for life renewal, for justice, for truth. And that is the answer to "why."

BECOMING A LIVING EXAMPLE FOR OTHERS

Now, perhaps you have not undergone a deep tragedy. Not everyone on planet Earth has the same job to do, the same stance to take.

Perhaps you are in a position to create positive changes on your own accord, without tremendous loss. Perhaps you can contribute something of value out of gratitude for all you do have. So, do give, do find a way to help others at no one's expense. For this is love, this is a gift for humanity, the reward from those who have to those who have not.

Many people lose their fortunes because they are greedy and selfish. They turn their heads away from the less fortunate. They turn their hearts to stone. They seek not the wisdom they can gain as a result of their fortunes, the wisdom of caring at no expense, the wisdom to contribute simply because they can.

So they lose what they did have. Some experience financial loss. Others keep their money and material possessions but lose their health or a loved one. Yet they remain hardened within, seeking solace from a bottle or a handful of pills rather than suffering their pains and causing a shift in their perspective. Perhaps if they gave purely, from their heart, without need for self aggrandizement, recognition, glory, or notoriety, but giving so no one but the receiver knew of their gift, perhaps then they would feel a sense of self renewal, a sense of purpose to their life.

So do give. Do see how you can be an example for others on your abundant path so they too can seek within to give to those less fortunate. This is an important lesson for humanity.

Many do learn. Many learn only as a result of great sacrifice. Many do not consciously seek to experience such loss and devastation, but on a soul level, they can look back and see that there *was a purpose* to the pain after all.

Then there are others who do not need to experience any of the more severe hardships or tragedies in order to contribute toward humanity.

Many were born to do this. Some have great wealth, and they give from their hearts. This is the example of those with a past life in which the desire to give back or help could not be realized; in this life they are the great philanthropists.

It truly does not matter how the circumstance falls into your life. The only thing that matters is that you do seek to see how you fit into the greater scheme of things on this planet and to see your connection to so many others, even those you may never meet. Yet somehow you will touch their lives in profound ways.

This is the ripple effect. Your deeds, which stem from your heart, are brought forth to help others, perhaps nearby, perhaps oceans away. But you do have an effect once you seek to bring forth your contribution to humanity.

This is humanity's reward. This is empowering pain, the rewards and authentic empowerment everyone experiences from those who give.

You have a purpose in this life larger than you, larger than your sphere of friends and immediate concerns. Without even knowing it, you can be the answer to the prayers of loved ones or strangers.

To be an answer to a prayer is a gift to be treasured. So as difficult as it may be to treasure your tragedies, know that doing so is the seed of life renewal. It is hope, justice, faith, and an answer for many. It is a gift that comes from the love and compassion of the precious few who know or have known the "dark night of the soul" and who found that even there, exists light.

Find the light within. In doing so, you raise your consciousness. Your purpose emerges. And what a grand gift you become: a beacon of light for the many.

Find the light within and you will help uplift humanity, even if only by one answered prayer at a time.

Trust your path. Know that if you have experienced tragic times, the gift is there. When you discover it, you will know that the words I speak are truth. You will know when you see the light that truly exists within your very purpose, within your soul.

Trust your purpose. Do not turn away. Build a foundation you yourself can lean on first, and as this foundation comforts you and helps you see your way through the darkness, it will also be a foundation for others to turn to, for the greater good of all.

Foundations are built with the heart, and the love on which they are built is eternal. As love and truth are eternal, so too is your purpose. Your gifts, eternal through their rippling effect, can truly uplift an entire human race.

Find your light within, and bring it forth for your own highest good and as a foundation for the greater good of all. This genuine empowerment heals the pain.

PART III

EVOLVING SPIRITUALLY

8

BREAKING AWAY FROM THE MATERIAL WORLD

*E*volution is perhaps the greatest teacher of the material world. For to evolve, you must come to learn, discover, and treasure your very essence, the part of you that exists and thrives beyond your ego's need for material gain.

To evolve, you must look around and place a value, a significance, a price on that which exists outside of yourself, compared to that which exists solely within.

How does an incarnate being, who is surrounded by every material thing conceived of by the human imagination, who needs materials for survival – how does that being break away from a material world?

What does "breaking away from the material world" really mean, beyond an esoteric, vague statement, such as "being spiritual"? For one can be poor, live a desolate life in the woods, and yet be a very unspiritual person. One can have everything money can buy and be a very spiritual person.

JUDGING SELF AND OTHERS

To judge another based on material wealth, or its lack, is to judge falsely. To break away from the material world simply means to:

Disassociate your value judgment about
your own self or others
from anything outside of yourself,
your innermost being
or the innermost being of another.

In today's society, greed, violence, poverty, wealth, freedom, imprisonment, glory, fame, notoriety, stature, and sometimes even life and death are too often determined by the magnitude of a person's material accumulation. Why should a materially wealthy person who commits murder roam free while another who has no material wealth is wrongfully placed on death row?

Why should the kidnapping of a child from a wealthy family be publicized and not that of a poor child? Why should the child of homeless parents be forced to live in the streets?

You see, this society does *not* value human beings just because they breathe with life or just because they have a heart, feelings, a purpose, lessons to learn, and gifts to share.

This society determines the value of human beings mainly by their material stature. Instead of integrating all people into one family of humanity, we pit one group against another: the haves against the have-nots.

People spend their lives working to buy the American dream: that big home, all the furnishings, the fancy car. They work, go into debt, and worry until they are so absorbed in trying to keep up or preventing losses and so exhausted by their unending efforts that they fight with their loved ones. Eventually, because of this stress, they destroy what they truly did cherish most: their family. The house, the media center, the car, all those things can be replaced, but a loved one cannot. I would ask you what price you would put on a loved one, but I am afraid some of you would actually have an answer. So I will refrain from asking the question, but I tell you that *no* price in this universe can be placed on a single life. Every life is priceless and irreplaceable.

Once you "get there," to the other side of your material goals, you will discover that the grass is certainly not greener on the other side, as it appeared to be.

The weeds of stress take over. The threat of drowning in debt becomes a reality. You may feel the cost of getting there via failing health, a frail nervous system, or a home life spiraling into the pits of negativity.

Many a millionaire has committed suicide. And many a poor person has helped to uplift humanity.

To break free from the material world, you have to honestly assess your relation to it and discover where you place your value as a human being.

Ask yourself: What circumstances, what conditions, what things make me feel truly worthy?

Then, imagine stripping away everything you named until you are left with nothing but your birthday suit. Do you *still* believe you are worthy?

The answer, I hope, is a hearty yes. Unfortunately, for the majority of the human population, the answer would be a screaming no.

Now, I am not saying you have to be naked to feel you are of value. You are entitled to have a home, conveniences, boats, planes, cars, anything and everything that brings joy or pleasure to your life. It is wonderful to have these things.

Yet having or not having these things must not be the basis of how you judge the worth of yourself or another. If it is, or ever has been, you have judged incorrectly. For all human beings can acquire or lose any *thing* that exists outside of their essence.

Self-worth or self-esteem
Cannot come from the outside in.
It can only come from the inside out.

Many have spoken of or written about the material world as an illusion. Material things are *not* an illusion. They are in front of your eyes; they do exist. The illusion is that any one thing outside of yourself determines your value or worth.

People may say, "Oh, he is very rich, he lives in a mansion, he is a very important person." Yet, this "very important person" may beat his wife and children every week. How important does that make him? How much better is he than the kind, loving farmer who plows his fields each day at sunrise?

The illusion is that your life, worth,
esteem, importance, or contribution to humanity
is based on material things.
This *is the* illusion.

Most people placed a very high value on Mother Teresa. They accurately assessed a very special human life. Yet how many material things did she own? She had very little, yet she helped to truly uplift humanity. She was a very special soul, doing much needed work. In fact, she was the epitome of an important person.

We all value virtue when we see it. Yet we lose sight of virtue in the face of a daily barrage of ads for material things that we are falsely led to believe will make us better people, more worthy, more highly respected – as if our intrinsic value were not enough to make us worthy and deserving of respect.

YOUR SOUL'S PERSPECTIVE, ALSO KNOWN AS THE BIG PICTURE

Removed yet divinely connected to our lives in this material world are our soul, our consciousness, and those aspects of our spiritual nature that exist simultaneously in this physical life and in the nonphysical realm – a parallel universe or other dimensions of this universe that would be called the fourth and fifth dimensions, where there are parallel realities and where there exists a "future self."

Now for many of you, this may seem like hogwash. And that's fine. Your perceptions can indeed remain solely in the third dimension of Earth, and you do *not* need to consider any reality other than the one you physically live in. *This is genuinely fine.*

For those of you who wish to expand on your current concept of self, however, this information may benefit your awareness of self and may help you to know how the other aspects of your soul relate to you, with your experiences being most valuable.

Your soul, that part of your being which knows no time or space, sees the higher perspective of the events that transpire in your everyday life.

This information is communicated to you while you sleep, and in many cases you receive communications in your dreams that seem to renew your perceptions upon waking in the morning and give you some sense of peace amid the pain and turmoil you face in your everyday life.

Those communications help you realize that your experiences are woven into the fabric and purpose of your entire life. The colors of some of those experiences may seem black and gloomy, yet when you look at the overall tapestry, you can see that the black is quite necessary: it provides contrast and brings more dimension, perspective, and even beauty to the other colors in your life.

This overall picture is what your soul sees. Your higher self, your soul, sees the black or bleak days you encounter simply as one part of your experience and not the beginning, middle, or end of your life. That is why the saying "This too shall pass" carries so much hope when we are faced with events that challenge our very spirit to persevere, even if only one moment at a time.

Now, as the fabric of your life is woven, at each step you face a choice. If you were to weave a pattern in a large tapestry, you would get a general idea of how the whole would turn out.

So when you seek an answer regarding the future, you receive an answer based on the energy vibrations you emit, along with a higher perspective of the energy from those connecting to your life who may be related to your question.

Now, at *any* point, you may choose a new path, a new pattern for your tapestry; this may or may not change the outcome.

The most important thing you must know is that you hold the individual power to choose how you respond to the events in your life; it is solely *your* choice to move in one direction or another. With your choices, you create your own reality.

Now, there are agreements between souls who enter your life for certain growth lessons or experiences in which you agreed to participate; those meetings are predestined, but their outcomes are not. The outcomes depend on the choices you make.

So, if you find you are being disempowered due to meeting a certain person, then consider that the reason this person entered your life was so you could grow to honor your own self and push away from one who undermines your growth, if you *choose* to do this. Should you choose to remain with one who undermines your growth and causes you to feel less than the incredible being you are, you will find that your choice results in misery. You will end up sacrificing your life, playing victim to a chance meeting, a meeting that was predestined to help you come to terms with your highest growth issue.

Of the millions of people who *are* sacrificing their very lives by choosing to remain in abusive relationships, all in the name of love, I ask, *Who* are you loving? Where are you keeping yourself, and what justifications are you using to avoid your own personal growth?

Do not use love as an excuse here. To be a victim, to falsely empower an abuser, is anything but love. To break away from this material world, to see your way beyond the challenges, you must set your sights above them and find the inner resources, by connecting to your higher self, to guide you in the direction of your choosing, for your highest good.

You see, God, your higher self, or whatever you believe in as a higher source of wisdom or consciousness in your life will never make your choices *for* you. This would take away *your* ability to choose your own direction, your own tapestry, and would empower another rather than strengthen you to determine your future based solely on your intentions.

As many of the souls living on earth now can attest, a part of your soul, your energy, lives a parallel life. To you, that life might seem like the future, but on the soul level, it is simultaneous. You *do*, however, have what you would call a future self.

When you ask for guidance about a certain situation in your life, you will be helped to create a reality in your best interest. You will also be warned of any potential repercussions should it appear that your choices do not serve the goal you strive for.

If you receive the guidance you asked for but do not follow it, you will find yourself feeling regret, find yourself having to go back to square one. So do yourself a favor and follow your guidance! Many of you channel, see visions, do writings, psychically receive information, or intuitively "know" something. But because your ego is only concerned with gratifying itself in the moment, your ego fights with your higher knowing or guidance to sway you, to cause you to give in to what may satisfy you in the moment. This prevents you from receiving the good you seek.

Many of you *doubt* your information, yet it is real. Only after repeated, observable accounts do you say, "OK, now I know this is real. I will follow my guidance." Once you do, you find your path to be so much easier, far less painful – because the perspective given to you is the highest perspective; it comes from your higher self or future self, so it knows exactly how to get from where you are at this moment to wherever or whatever your goal is.

Another part of the "illusion" is that there exists no other universe but planet Earth and no other type of being except humanity, which still has not evolved beyond the level of people shooting each other on a highway or taking a piece of gold in exchange for a human life. The thought that this is the highest evolved species in this universe is a concept created only by your ego. There are civilizations far more advanced in every possible way, civilizations far more loving, compassionate, and cooperative, and that is *why* they are more evolved.

After this life on earth, a small percentage of you may choose to reincarnate into another life on earth to help the human species; or you may choose to remain in the fourth dimension because your energy vibration has truly risen above the negative density of the third dimension. Either way, your choices are before you, and we do take one life at a time.

The part of your soul that experiences life as what you would call your future self can and does transfer information back to you, because you share the energy of one vast soul. Therefore you *can* know what to do and how to get from one point in your life to another, but your intentions *must* be of the purest form, solely of love and light. As many of you already know, the more spiritually evolved you are, the more and the faster any intention of malice backfires. You are far too aware, and you pay a dear price for *any* negative intention or action. Therefore, purity of thought, word, and deed is of the utmost importance when you are trying to manifest something in your life.

The universe will literally rush in to help you when your motive or intention is to be of help or service, or when you seek to manifest something of love in your life, so long as it truly serves your highest good and can ultimately serve the highest good of all.

Many of you who are involved with your soul mates will find that the energy you share, once combined, is truly an unstoppable force for so much good not only for your own personal bliss but for that of all people. So when you go against the current of your own energy, you feel as if you are fighting a raging river, and this is both exhausting and painful. Much better is to go with the flow of your natural current, in the direction of your natural energy, which is seeking to bring you farther along on the path of your own chosen evolution. You see, stagnation hurts. All human beings feel so much more alive when they strive to be or simply are their own personal best. When you settle for less than your best, you know it. This erodes your self-esteem. It never enhances it.

So as you ask for a solution or guidance to help move in a positive direction in your life, trust that your guidance, wisdom, or newfound clarity is coming from your higher self. Much information is sent to you from your future self as well. All communicate, all give and receive information, which is trans-muted into thought patterns or energy frequencies that reach you in a way you can easily decipher. Once you get a consistent ex-change going, the communication becomes clearer, more precise, and more easily understood.

For when you communicate to your higher self, it is as if you have an energy frequency tuned to one wave, like a radio station. Your higher self, your future self, your soul is always tuned into you, but some effort is required for you to tune in, so the energy exchange or frequency can be adjusted, like a radio dial, for the precise frequency that can result in a clear back-and-forth con-nection, easily heard and understood, to the point that it has a positive, expansive, and significant effect in your life, all of your own asking. Of course, whether or not you follow your guidance is up to you.

So, if you have opened up your ability to communicate with that part of your soul which can see the big picture, the tapestry, please trust that you are not making it all up. Your energy vibra-tion is higher than it was earlier in your life, when perhaps you were not as open to your multisensory communication, so it may feel as if it is coming from "just you," and it truly is. It is coming from that part of you which exists outside the material world, yet simultaneously experiences your life in the material world.

To break away from the material world, your consciousness must be expanded enough to know that your life is but a part of the tapestry of your soul's existence.

An event in your life is only a part of your life and not your whole life.

Do keep the grander picture in mind. Keep the perspective that any event or circumstance or person in your life does not constitute your entire life but a part of it.

This can be either most pleasurable or most painful. I would venture to say that any experience that brings you pain is there for you to grow and learn from. Moreover, any experience that brings you pleasure is given to you because you deserve to experience pleasure.

Do seek to grow and to learn so all of your life can be as joyful and as pleasurable as possible.

Suffering is part of the tapestry until you realize the gift or the *reason* for the suffering. In most cases suffering stems from denial of what is in front of you and from your fear of embracing that which is trying to move you in the most positive direction. So, as you suffer, you are forced to look at the source of your suffering. It is not the other. It is you. And it is your choice to either embrace the experiences before you or walk away from them. You will know which course of action will ultimately bring you the greatest happiness. When you are true to yourself, you always know what to do.

This is paramount in a consciousness, a life that seeks to evolve.

Your potential is unlimited as a human being.

Your existence within the material world is before you to discover who you truly are in relation to all that is around you. Are you greedy or generous? Passionate or coldly indifferent? Compassionate or angry?

You choose, in relation to all that surrounds you.

To break free from the negative cycle so many on earth engage in, you turn within to find your highest perception of self. And you find that you are connected not only to all of humanity but to a vast universe you have yet to see. Yet, aspects of your soul exist in parallel universes and communicate with you because your energy is vast, and you are so much more than you realize today in this earthbound, material existence.

You are a part of the cosmos that awaits you, a universe in which you will experience every aspect of your being.

See the grander picture, the whole tapestry. Do not ever become so negative or caught up in what many call the cosmic joke: the trials of petty everyday circumstances, the traffic tickets, traffic in general, a job, a credit report, a house. All of these things are transient. You, however, are eternal. Your soul knows no bound-aries and neither should you.

The truth is, you have no boundaries. That is the illusion. See beyond the circumstances before you. Ask for help. You receive assistance every moment. Your life, your soul, does not take the microcosm of your daily experience as seriously as your ego does. It looks to the macrocosm, and there it finds peace.

When you spill water on your business suit, you may get upset. But when you look out over the vast ocean, you feel peace.

Such is the peace of a higher perspective. Seeing the big picture helps to ease the tears of the day. It shows how each drop is neces-sary for the whole, and the whole of your life can be achieved only by choosing to see the beauty within each day. Each moment is equated with a drop of the most peaceful ocean water. Treasure your moments whether they come from rain, tears, or the fine mist of morning dew. For each drop will never be separate from the whole of your life, yet it is not the whole of your life. Choose the perspective that brings peace to your heart. Choose the level of awareness that sees beyond the ordinary and brings you into the extraordinary where you belong, simultaneously within yet broken away from the material world.

Don't take it all so seriously, yet treasure every nuance. Bring the highest and best out from within your own being, for this is the only way you can truly serve. If you each do this, then ulti-mately the paths of many will share a richer, more peaceful expe-rience within the tapestry of humanity.

9   SPIRITUAL CONSCIOUSNESS

For concepts and theories regarding spirituality or spiritual consciousness to be useful, they must be clear and understandable, and there must be simple ways to apply them in one's inner and outer life.

When I say inner life, I mean within your heart and mind. By outer life, I mean your everyday experiences.

Unlike others, I cannot endorse as appropriate for all situations such phrases as "love another as you love yourself" or "turn the other cheek." Although these sayings are often useful, obviously they have not reached the masses in a way that hits home. As a result, they have not had a positive effect on people's everyday lives.

People often misinterpret such phrases at their own expense. For example, if a man strikes his girlfriend or wife, she must not turn the other cheek; she must not cite those words to justify excusing his behavior because to do so clearly does not show love of self.

So, what is spiritual consciousness, and how can it be applied to your life simply and logically?

Spiritual consciousness is love and truth combined with the inner strength to display them in your actions.

Spiritual consciousness is the highest ideal you can strive to attain in every moment of your life: to be true to yourself, to love yourself enough to live your truth no matter how it may temporarily hurt, and to walk your talk without fear.

Here is a simple example: Your life is like a river, with bends, twists, calm, turbulence, and all kinds of experiences along the way. When your actions match your thoughts and feelings, your truth, the ride down this river is an enriching experience.

Now imagine riding down the river with one leg in one canoe labeled your genuine thoughts and feelings, and the other leg in another canoe labeled your actions. When you feel something in your heart and think something in your mind, but your spoken words do not reflect that truth, the two canoes separate, pulling your legs apart as you ride the river of your life. This is a most painful way to travel, and the simple truth is that it is unnecessary.

If you applied this concept to every area of your life, starting today, your life would certainly make a dramatic turnaround because you would genuinely be living your truth.

To do this, first acknowledge every aspect of your life in which your actions or words are not congruent with your genuine thoughts and feelings. Next, place all of those aspects in an imaginary basket. Then, one by one, resolve those aspects or get rid of them once and for all.

Suppose you are not truly happy with your job but you continue to go to this place of employment day in and day out. Put the job in the basket, find a better one more in line with what you love to do, and toss out the old job.

You may have financial debt. Put all your bills into the basket and one by one make a payment arrangement to clear them up.

You may be in a long-term relationship; perhaps the one you love has been sitting on the fence, causing you a lot of pain. You can never demand that others do something they are not ready for, but you can make your own decision to either continue living with the pain of settling for less than you deserve or to walk to the other side of the fence alone. When you do that, you clear the way for someone else to enter your life. You may even make it possible for the one you love to get off the fence and commit to the truth in his heart, if he genuinely loves you.

You see, it takes courage to live your truth, to be honest with yourself and show it. It is far easier, and far more painful, to feel one way and behave in another.

Why is this called spiritual consciousness? Because it provides the impetus to get in touch with the deepest part of your innermost being, the true core of you and you alone. When you bring your essence, your truth, out from within and up to the surface of your life, then you can see and feel the real you in all your life experiences.

When you do this, you glow. You awaken your own vitality. Your unique inner spirit comes forth and shines in every part of your life.

Your consciousness, which is your mind, intelligence, intuition, and wisdom, marries that inner essence, which is your unique, individual expression. It is the flour and water combined that makes the wonderful bread.

Self-truth causes us to face things we would rather avoid. Yet, after enduring the pain of traveling down the river of life with each leg in a different canoe simultaneously moving in opposite directions, at some point we make the decision to bring the two together. From this point forward we find peace. Our inner life matches our outer life. We say how we really feel. We speak what we honestly think. We do what we know to be right, true, genuine, and good for us and others. We stop avoiding the truth and find the guts to live it and express it no matter how it may temporarily bruise our own ego or someone else's.

This is taking individual power to the pinnacle of performance; this will transform every obstacle life offers.

If you believe in your heart that you want something, your actions will take you in the direction of your goal one step at a time. Conversely, if you desire to achieve something, and you do not do what it takes to reach that goal no matter how difficult it may be, then your legs are back in two separate canoes moving in two different directions along the river of your life. This is no way to travel. It is painful and gets you nowhere.

The current of a river changes moment to moment and day to day. You cannot go backwards and duplicate yesterday's path. You cannot live with regret, wallowing at the turn you didn't take prior to this moment. You have to begin where you are now and ride the river of the rest of your life moment to moment, with your canoes aligned. Then and only then will you ultimately get where you want to be.

So if life brought a storm, and the ride was miserable, okay; now what are you going to do?

If you believe you can have a better life, you are right! Match your belief with your actions, and your journey will surely take you there.

If you believe this is it and there can be no change, no benefit, growth, opportunity, or learning, then you do not realize you are traveling on a river. You have managed to convince yourself you are in your grave. Only in your grave can you never again turn your life around. Of course if you were really in your grave, you would not be reading these words. So whether it is one small area of your life or many areas, decide first where the problem lies, what erroneous pattern you have repeated, or where you have neglected to take personal responsibility and action, and begin to change your path. Today.

Although we cannot plan every twist and turn, and although we may not know that a certain bend in the river will take us on a more rewarding path toward our highest ideals, we can certainly prepare for the journey by focusing each day on where we would like to go and dealing with each twist as it arises, with truth, while our actions match that truth.

We can cry, we can feel great fear, but remember that those emotions are transient, not eternal. Self-truth, however, is eternal. So as long as we behave in a way that mirrors our deepest truths and not those of ego, anger, or fear in the moment, we get in touch with the truth beneath it all. And it becomes easier to walk a genuine talk rather than be scattered by momentary winds that pass.

As you grow, you may genuinely change from within, and then your truth changes. People who have grown will change different aspects of their lives. As they grow with wisdom and learn valuable lessons, their outer lives reflect a new inner truth. Their identity does not change with each blowing wind.

Even during the course of writing this book, I have found that the hardest thing to do is to confront a meaningful area of my life from the core of my being, where truth resides. Often there is the potential of losing something or someone we hold dear. Yet I knew that if I were ever to know genuine inner peace, I would have to learn to hold myself dearest of all, to truly be my own best friend, and to risk living my truth through my actions.

So you may find that being honest with yourself is difficult. It is scary and painful. Yet the eternal saying still carries all of the wisdom in the world: "The truth shall set you free."

No matter what you try to have, do, be, bring into your life, make better, or release from your life, as long as your efforts genuinely match your truth and your motive is purely to live your truth, then ultimately you will indeed have what you need. As you live your truth, you will refuse to settle for less than what you know, deep inside, is best for you.

If you do settle for less, then you are not living your truth. You are, once again, riding your river with each leg in a different canoe, where pain is the only possible result.

There is a saying I learned along my life journey: "You cannot serve two masters." You cannot serve love and fear at the same time. You cannot serve truth and fallacy at the same time.

So at each step, for each decision, you must make a choice.

After giving in to fear or fallacy over and over again and finally realizing the river of your life has taken you nowhere you truly want to be, you learn, as I have learned, that self denial, procrastination, and wimping out are not the truth.

Ultimately, you choose to be true to you. Your life then becomes a physical expression of your ideal you, one day, one experience, and one decision at a time. It is then and only then that you are genuinely free.

You refuse to settle, give in, or give up at the expense of you and your truth. Then you ride your river with joy, inner peace, and clarity of thought. Then you achieve the results you seek. Yes, this is the scariest part of life. It requires the most courage.

This is the only way, however, that you will transform every obstacle standing in your way, the only way you can finally live the life you have always dreamed of.

After practice, it gets easier, less fearful, and far less painful. After dedicated, consistent perseverance, your life clearly becomes one celebrated victory after another – the victory of your own individual power to clear every obstacle and enjoy every moment of the life you have created.

Our journeys are sometimes filled with many tears, and it is often when we reach within to the core of our own truth that we feel our deepest pain. Honor and love the pain. Learn from it. Know very clearly it will certainly heal over time.

Letting go of old beliefs, patterns, ego defenses, and the false fronts we put up to shield us from one very special person or from the rest of the world is painful; it leaves us bare, with the naked truth. But from this point forward, we can free ourselves of every obstacle that has blocked us from what we truly seek within the deepest part of us.

Each day, the newfound truth strengthens us; it becomes our rock, our comfort, our backer, cheerleader, and best friend. For to become one's own best friend, everything that is not true for one's self must yield to the truth.

From this point we build the most enriching, rock-solid foundation to strengthen us and keep us intact no matter how stormy life becomes.

Dare to be real. Dare to live your truth, and dare to go forward. When you do, every obstacle standing between you and deep happiness will finally melt away.

AFTERWORD

I thought I had finished this book. I believed I had said all I have learned. Then I picked up Debbie Ford's book *The Dark Side of the Light Chasers*. Oh boy, did I have more healing to do. I discovered this when I completed one of the exercises in that book. It directed me to connect with that part within which contains the highest self truths, my "sacred self," and ask: "What [do] you need to do to open your heart and let go of any emotional toxicity you have been carrying around?"

With pen and journal in hand, I began writing. I will now transcribe those words from my personal journal because I believe with all my heart that they were not just for me but for you as well.

You are filled with love, self-love, with the permission to love self. And you have no issue anymore with love. You are loved, you are love, you love others, and they love you, as a soul, as a human being. Love flows freely in and out and all around your life, and now you embrace this love, realizing it was always there. Realizing that you had to discover it for you, not from another, but from within your self, your heart, your soul, and this love of self sets you free from the need or the fear or the compromises you never need to make.

Can a light say: "I need light. I am afraid I won't be light or have light or get light or be worthy of light"? Can a lit candle say this? No! A lit candle is light. You, Barbara, are love! You always have been. But when you were small, you felt unloved. So the message was, "I am not lovable." So you began to search for love when it has been within you all of this time. The candle perhaps saw other candles go away. A Daddy candle went away. And the candle said: "I don't have light now. Where is light? How can I get light?" But all the while, the candle was light. All the while the little candle took the perception of Daddy candle or Mommy candle leaving as if light left her, when in actuality nothing, no light, no love left it, or you. You are no more worthless than a lit candle is lightless. And no other candle can give you what you already have: Light. Love, which is your make-up and has not changed although you thought it did, in the absence of a parent who a child was attached to. So when the parent went away, you believed a vital part of you was gone or ignored or not valued, not worthy. So for nearly forty years you have been trying to bring yourself what you have always had: Love. Seeking from others what you never realized was your essence: Love. Believing that a candle dressed in cool clothes or hanging out with other cool candles or being in a fancy house could ever make that candle any more or any less than it was. No, it would not. A candle is a candle, filled with light. A person is a person, filled with love. So once the deception stops, the door is opened to your true self. This is true Individual Power. This is what Transforms Every Obstacle: Love. Love of self and for self, because it is only truth that will heal the lies, and it is only the light of the truth that will show the path toward authentic transformation. And that path is pure love.

You are the candle, and you are loved. The candle is light, and the light is a light for oneself.

So there it is, directly from my personal journal. I finally get it, from within. We have to experience understanding ourselves in order to heal ourselves. I finally *feel* the peace I have sought my entire life.

I am deeply grateful to Debbie Ford, whom I have not yet met, for sharing herself and her healing process so that I was able to continue mine. Thank you.

I do hope that now you can see the true power in giving and sharing. They are not simply esoteric concepts reserved for the few. They are the connection we all share, the connection that transforms each of us individually and thus transforms all of humanity when we give ourselves permission to simply be ourselves.

I have spoken much about letting go of fears when seeking to manifest something, and I have talked about embracing a challenge no matter how tragic or painful it may appear to be.

How does one genuinely do this? With hindsight, I realized that I always saw the gift as a result of an unpleasant circumstance. I also looked back and realized how hard I fought to hold on to what I did not want to change in my life. Trying to keep the status quo is not transforming an obstacle into an opportunity. It is delaying or trying to stop the realization of an opportunity, no matter how much we think we do not want it.

Our egos will fight, but ultimately, our highest purpose and the wisdom of our soul will win. That explains the cliché, "Everything always works out in the end." Sometimes it works out after much fighting on our part. But with age comes wisdom. As I am now completing four decades, I can share the wisdom of this process with you.

Move into the area you fear most. Tell yourself: "No matter how I may be fighting this now, the gifts of this experience will emerge over time. No matter how much my fearful personality fights this experience, I can see from past experience that something happened for reasons I was unable to see at the time. For the first time, I am going to trust, even if it is for only a second at a time. I am going to allow this river to take me where I probably wanted to wind up anyway but did not know exactly how to get there. Life knows."

We cannot know everything at every turn. That is why so many of us hold on to our current realities so tightly. The unknown is out of the ego's domain. It is the domain of the soul, filled with wisdom and gifts. The only domain of the ego is the past. A prior point of reference, based on the experiences we have already lived. We want to evolve, however, not stagnate in our own history.

You will find that as you move willingly into the experience staring you in the face, a lot of the pain and anxiety lessens. You may even begin to see the gifts offered as a result of the experience a lot faster, which of course will only help you.

I love analogies. So here is mine. Back to the river:

You are on this wild river of your life. The river is your life. You have a goal or a number of them. You have dreams, hopes, wishes, and a life purpose. They all intertwine. You think something is supposed to happen at a certain time or in a certain way as you ride along. Then comes the bend in the river. The current takes you in what you think is a different direction. You grab onto a branch dangling from a tree, and you hold on for dear life. You fight, cry, bargain with God, resist, avoid, and fight, fight, fight the current with every ounce of fearful strength your personality has to offer.

What you or your personality or your ego can not see is that this bend is taking you exactly where you truly wanted to go. But you are so busy fighting it all and holding on that it is only after you let go that you realize it. Maybe you let go two years later. Maybe twenty. I hope you will let go at the onset of this bend in the river and move with the current rather than fight it. Then you will realize how necessary this bend is to get you where you want to be.

I just experienced this in my own life. Letting go was the hardest thing for me. I always wanted to feel in control. I fought until I was left with no choice. And then, I was grateful. Or I understood. Or I realized all of the reasons why.

We will always discover the reasons in hindsight, but with this process, we can see them from the beginning, and that truly transforms the obstacles our fears create for us.

Move into the experience you are fighting so hard to avoid. The gifts are there!

I wish you every joy and beauty life offers, and I wish that you discover where it truly resides: within you.

REGARDING CHILD CUSTODY

While writing this book, I marked the six-year anniversary of my custody battle. I have learned vital lessons that I want to share with all parents.

Our children are not to be fought over like property. Children are not property, and parents do not own them. The issue is not custody. It is loving the children, sharing parental responsibility for their physical needs, and maintaining open communication between the parents *for the sake of* the children.

If you file a custody suit out of bitterness, or to get personal revenge, or to avoid sharing parental responsibility with open communication, you commit a crime against your children.

No matter how much you may despise your former spouse, your children are as much a part of their other parent as they are of you. No matter how much you may dread sharing open, healthy communication with your former spouse, you must do it to provide a role model of healthy adult communication for your children; they will need this vital resource when they become adults.

Psychologically healthy divorced parents show courtesy and respect to each other. Their children then internalize the message that they are respected. Through open dialogue with each other, parents teach their children to speak their truth rather than sacrifice it to please one parent or blame the other. Such parents give their children an invaluable gift.

When parents stop blaming and start to look within, they take personal responsibility for their thoughts, feelings, and actions. The parents heal their issues, and their children are spared great pain.

I ask you, if you are a parent, to look to the source of your pain. It is not with your former spouse. It is within you. Look closely at the areas you vehemently guard. If you don't want open communication, do it anyway. Your children need to learn how to communicate. If you don't want to pay child support, pay it anyway. Your children are entitled to be raised with the financial resources of both parents. They deserve the best life they can possibly have.

Do everything you do not want to do. Do it for your children. If you do, your children will be by your side in your old age. If you do not, you will find yourself alone when you are old.

My mother divorced my natural father when I was five years old. He avoided child support. He moved to another state. He loved me dearly, but he was too caught up in his own issues with my mother to overlook them and be there for me. I missed out on sharing my life with my natural father. He misses the joy of knowing his grandchildren today. The man I regard as my father now is the one who adopted me and raised me. Despite his old ways, he too has learned, grown, and healed.

Many laws have changed in the last thirty-five years: child support enforcement laws and custody regulations. But the courts cannot enforce healthy, open communication between the parents. And the courts cannot impose on us the one thing that will make all the difference for each of us. It comes from the inside. It is love.

Love and heal your self. Love and honor your children. Then and only then will you and your children know peace.

APPENDIX

A Call to Action from Barbara Rose and American People for Family Justice-Child Legislation

*B*elow are three letters that I fervently hope you will send to your elected representatives and senators in Washington, D.C. You can copy the letters and mail them as is, or you can add anything you want to say regarding the issues. Be sure to include your full name and address, or your letter will be ignored. Elected representatives usually respond only to their own constituents.

It is my deepest hope that the three bills described in the letters will be enacted into law.

Your voice is vital in stamping out the injustice perpetrated on innocent children and replacing it with justice. Your help can make all the difference in the world. Thank you for your support.

Letter #1 endorsing the Post-Dissolution Primary Caregiver Act proposed by American People for Family Justice-Child Legislation

Dear _____:

Please support the Family Justice Post-Dissolution Primary Caregiver Act and do all you can to have it enacted into law.

The travesty of unwarranted and unjust child custody suits has caused unnecessary pain and life-long scars for countless parents and children.

When a primary caregiver/primary custodial/residential parent of minor children has previously been established as such upon dissolution of marriage, and the minor children have been living with their primary parental caregiver, they are presumed to be in the safe, loving care of this parent.

Unfortunately many non-custodial parents seek custody for ulterior motives, such as revenge against a former spouse or avoidance of child-support obligations.

Most single parents cannot afford to pay for experienced legal representation throughout the custody litigation process. Furthermore, many custody cases are unwarranted and cause an unnecessary burden on the family court system.

To prevent unjust custody battles and unnecessary trauma to children, the Family Justice Post-Dissolution Primary Caregiver Act states that custody litigation cannot be pursued unless it has first been determined that children are in danger and that there is sufficient cause to remove the children from their primary parental caregiver.

The state can perform physical and psychological assessments to determine if the children are in danger. If it is found that the primary caregiver/custodial parent does not present any danger to the children, then there is no need to pursue custody litigation. If the children are, in fact, found to be in danger, then a change in custody or primary residence could be warranted, and custody litigation would proceed.

The Family Justice Post-Dissolution Primary Caregiver Act will protect children from unnecessary pain and psychological abuse often inflicted on them by parents who are antagonistic toward each other, and will prevent the psychological trauma and emotional scars that could result from such pain and abuse. The children's home life will remain stable.

The Family Justice Post-Dissolution Primary Caregiver Act will prevent primary caregivers/custodial parents from losing primary responsibility/custody of their children without just cause even if they cannot afford to pay for continuous legal representation.

Many single parents sue for custody years after divorce. There are no legal protections in place to prevent innocent custodial parents from being railroaded within the system due to lack of finances for exorbitant legal fees. The children are used as pawns by far too many parents who want to "win" or "get back at" their former spouse. This is a crime against the children.

As your constituent, I urge you to rally bipartisan support of this gender-neutral act for the well-being of children and for justice for loving single parents who perpetrated no wrongdoing whatsoever upon their children but cannot afford to defend themselves.

Sincerely,

Name _____

Address _____

_____

City, State_____Zip _____

Letter #2 endorsing the Child Protection from Foster Care Act proposed by American People for Family Justice-Child Legislation

Dear _____:

Children may be sexually molested, abused, and neglected while in the foster-care system. Sometimes they die.

The Child Protection from Foster Care Act would protect children from being removed from the care of guardian relatives other than their parents and placed into foster care unless it is shown by physical and psychological tests that the relatives are causing harm to the children.

If the relative inadvertently breaks a court order or does something else that brings no harm to the child, the child will remain in the care of the family member and will not be traumatized by being placed in the foster-care system.

I urge you to rally bipartisan support for this act to protect children from being removed needlessly from the loving care of family members and placed into a foster-care system that can result in life-long psychological scars.

Sincerely,

Name _____

Address _____

_____

City, State_____Zip _____

Letter #3 endorsing the Child Custody Counseling Act proposed by American People for Family Justice-Child Legislation

Dear _____:

Countless minor children have been abused and harmed by a parent. After divorce, residential custody of these children may be changed to the other parent or to another primary caregiver.

Countless other minor children have been in the safe and loving care of their primary parent after divorce. As a result of unjust custody battles, however, children are sometimes needlessly removed from the loving care of their primary parent.

In all cases, the children suffer emotional scars and pain. They need emotional counseling to heal, adjust, and cope with their life-altering circumstances so that they do not carry psychological scars into their teen years and adult life.

Unresolved emotional pain experienced during childhood is known to be a large contributing factor to teen violence.

Innocent children deserve to receive emotional counseling to heal the pain that was unjustly perpetrated on them.

I urge you to rally bipartisan support to enact into law the Child Custody Counseling Act. This act would ensure that any child who is removed from the custody of one parent or primary caregiver and placed into the physical custody of another parent or primary caregiver, no matter what the circumstances, receive three to six months of private psychological counseling to be paid for by the primary custodial caregiver.

Sincerely,

Name _____

Address _____

_____

City, State_____Zip _____

Printed in the United States
63031LVS00002B/101